THE
50 STEPS *to*
HAPPY MARRIAGE

THE 50 STEPS *to* HAPPY MARRIAGE

(*A Life Positioning System – Lps*)

Anthony O. Nwachukwu

Library of Congress Control Number: 2019907614

PAPERBACK: 978-1-7332264-5-5
EBOOK: 978-1-7332264-6-2

Ordering Information:

For orders and inquiries, please contact:
1-888-404-1388
www.goldtouchpress.com
book.order@goldtouchpress.com

Printed in the United States of America

CONTENTS

DEDICATION

This Marriage Guide is dedicated to all those who make honest efforts to live in peace with one another, be it in the married state or other states in life.

FOREWORD

Human management is most difficult because every person tends to behave true to type. Forging interpersonal relationships among married couples makes even greater demands because of the degree of commitment involved: a total and mutual self-donation that is for life. This project is not made easier given the fact that the two parties come from different cultural milieu to build a community of love and life.

Given the abounding cases of breakups, instability and divorce in many marriages in our society today, I consider the present work at hand very apt and timely. The author may not have been an expert in the area of marriage. Yet, his contributions so far, may remain a *hand book of marriage instructions* for both the married and the unmarried people, especially in this 21st Century.

Therefore, while I congratulate Fr. Anthony for this masterpiece, I do recommend that all may avail themselves of this wonderful opportunity, hoping that it will go a long way to assisting couples to successful and happy married lives.

Rev. Fr. Dr. M. Elekwachi

Defensor Vinculi
Ahiara Diocesan Marriage Tribunal
Former Lecturer: Seat of Wisdom Seminary,
Owerri, Imo State.

ACKNOWLEDGMENT

To
God, the author of Marriage,
My Mother, Mary, Ever Blessed Virgin,
Leaders of the Spiritual (Church) and Temporal World,
Divine Soldiers on the battle field of Faith, Men and Women,
Married and Single Family Members and Friends,
Men and Women of Good Conscience
Adults and Minors,
Religious, Spiritual and Non-Religious,
Experts whose works have been cited here, et cetera,
Thank You All!

SPECIAL PROMOTIONAL BLURBS FROM MARRIED COUPLES

In a special way, I acknowledge your contributions in this work and encouragements to me. Don't be offended if I failed to reflect yours as well!

Part of the personal letter of Mrs. Philo I. Ekanem to me – Former National President, National Catholic Council of Women Organization of Nigeria (N.C.C. W.O.N).: "I congratulate you, Fr. Anthony, on your beautiful booklets, just out, worthy Son .... Both booklets are very interesting and enriching";

For her Excellency, Prof., Viola Adaku Onwuliri, former Nigeria's minister of education and foreign affairs, author and women leader: "Marriage is an honest surrender of 'part of self' to each other, in an unconditional love, active service, devoted prayer-life and total resolve to the plan of God". Teach your children to know and love God first, and you will have no worries of their future".

For Ngozi Igwilo and husband (USA), "Marriage is heaven-bound but celebrated on earth. Thus, fidelity in marriage is totally divine and obliges every partner to comply".

A human rights activist, based in the USA, Princess Winnie Obi, and for her: "Marriage is one of the finest and sacred institutions ordained by God, and I believe and respect it as such. It differs from all other relationships".

Madam Malam, the current President (at the time of first publication), noted: "Congrats Fr. Nwachukwu for enlightening us in our tough vocations!"

Prof. D.A. Onyejemezi - Dean, School of PG Studies, IMSU, said: "Fr. Anthony, you are wonderful, always enriching society spiritually with your write ups";

An Accountant, Mr. Stephen Onyia,(USA), praising his wife, Chika, for her meritorious awards, noted: "Marriage is reliability, sincerity and communication. Always be humble to apologize to each other when you are at fault. 'Talking out' has instantly helped us to resolve issues. Never take sides or team up against any family member when misunderstanding springs up in your house. Be firm to apportion blames fearlessly and justly".

Rev. Fr. Dr. Anthony Nwudah - Judicial Vicar, Ahiara Diocesan Marriage Tribunal (now in the USA): "Elder, I am very happy with your work, *The 50 Steps*; I read every line of it and alerted my Catechist. It will be used for marriage instructions."

From Rev. Fr. J.O. Ononiwu - former PP., C.K.C., Okpala, now in U.S.A.: "Compliments of the season Fr. Anthony, and congratulations for your book, *The Devil Has Come To Church*, more grease to your elbows";

For Dr. Festus E. Ngumah, Chairman, Pastoral Council, Ahiara Diocese, then, Chairman L.G.A. Service Commission, Imo State (Retired in the USA, but frequents Nigeria): "Marriage begins, first of all, with an agreement a man and a woman make to each other, be it in the traditional or ecclesial perspective";

From Anastasia, Ifeoma, the wife of Engr. Daniel Chukwuemeka Nwasokwa, Nursing Department, USA, for the couple: "Marriage is partnership galvanized – stimulated and enshrined in God's love and design. We daily look onto Him to direct and bless our little efforts".

For the Retired, but serving Deacon, Rev. O. Miranda of St. Fortunata Church, USA: "With time, in my 35 years of marriage, we grew in each other. Today, I know her likes and her dislikes, a knowledge that comes with lots of respect, love and sacrifices". Elaborating further, Rev. Osborne M. added: "Many of the joyous marriages being shown or advertised in the TV or social media today are not real". These are marriages in their preliminal stage, like the 'id' personality structure, as detailed in this life Guide to H/M, where questions are seldom, if at all, asked.

For Lady Julie Anyanwu - former Archdiocesan and Provincial President of the C.W.O: "No marriage can survive without prayer….and for any marriage to be successful, one partner must appear to be 'foolish' just to allow peace reign ….";

Mrs. Victoria Ibe of University of Agric, Umudike, commending her husband, Prof. S. N. Ibe of the same address, noted: "Only little, little things, just doing little things, for each other, has kept our marriage journey, smooth and moving. If my husband loves me today, or does anything for me, I am really instrumental to it";

From Pat – Tax Professional Services, NY: "What is most important in marriage is communication, so that the two partners may understand what each is thinking about their union/marriage at the moment".

For Lady Otigbuo, Mary – Former President, C.W.O. Aba Diocese: "Marriage for me is just tolerance, live and let live, allowing your partner to have his or her own non-harmful way, and avoid being greedy";

For Martha Caraballo, Secretary of The Most Precious Blood Parish, Astoria, NY: "Marriage is about caring for the other without hesitation. It is about unconditional love. I am a fan of the woman doing all to please the man; however, there is a limit. Marriage should be 50/50. One person should never do more than the other. In exasperation, it may seem more at times, but you should never count how many times you do something over, how many times the other person does things… Even though it may be your turn to do the chores, help one another out a little. A little goes a long way, and a lot faster. One cooks, one washes the dishes. One bathes the children; one dresses them, while the other gets them ready for bed. It doesn't have to be every day the same thing, change it up a little. Accept that the other is tired, and make it up. Nothing is ever perfect in life. To love someone, you must accept who they are and what they are and not want to change them. Accept them and they will accept you. 100% goes to God. You go to Church together; you pray together, do the rosary together. A happy life is a family of God.

INTRODUCTION

"What God has united man must not separate"
Mark 10:10.

We are all products of marital circumstances. This time around, I have picked my pen to arouse our consciousness on the issue that concerns all of us. Life is not only larger than logic but also a process, a Big Book, already marked. Only the Author knows the pages where it begins and ends! There is more to life than material possessions! Never compromise your standards of life – peace of mind, personal healthy life styles, choices and happiness with those of living – huge bank accounts and luxurious life styles etc! Relaxed human relationships come first! Your own life remains what you make out of it, mindful of the fact that "the mind can only absorb what the seat can endure". - Berg Joseph A. Be recollected! At the end, you are the pillar to your success or failure! Thus, this Marriage Guide enjoins us to be the best person, husband, wife or minister we can! Remember, each of us can be a hero somewhere! Prayerfully search for it in your other half, your helpmate, always rejoice with those who rejoice and sorrow with those who are deeply challenged, because as pilgrims, we are all home-bound!

Is it not alarming to record the frequency with which many marriages breakup these days, families torn to pieces? In the past when our forefathers practiced polygamy, there was peace, harmony in their families. Why do we have such sharp divisions in our Christian marriages today? Jean Paul Sartre seemed to have some clues when he remarked: "Everything has been figured out except how to live" (IR). To live is not the same thing as to exit. Partners in marriage, and not in sex, are meant to live in thanksgiving for a privileged relationship, which, if they cooperate, will always lead them to a fulfilled-joyful union with God and man, bearing in mind that the most effective and positive evaluation any partner can give to the other must begin from himself. For instance, if something is bothering you in your relationship, you must talk about it. Thus, these 50 interconnected and interwoven steps to Happy Marriage are the author's priestly heart-felt, prayerful wishes to all partners to reach and enjoy the Golden Jubilee of their union. The word "partner" is generically used in this Marriage Guide to include any person, who is engaged in one form of relationship or the other – in corporate setting, the lay, ordained or professed in any religious order. Do also remember that in marriage or other relationships, some steps may be tougher than the rest. Please, be careful! The application of male gender in many places here also incorporates the female. It was done for easy readability and comprehension. Any repetition here is solely for emphasis, including the use of "a couple" for "couples". The steps comprised of '3 stages' of marriage! There might be more or less! Partners can cozily settle down at the 1st step, the 2nd stage, climb more or navigate the 50 steps all together! The stages are the "Preliminal, Liminal and Postliminal". While the Preliminal is primarily the excitement stage, where fewer questions, if at all, are raised, and where marriage curiously appears to have reached its apogee, omega point or the high water mark of love – the core of self-identity, the Liminal is the 'reality stage' - the embodiment and examples of ideal relationships with gradual realization of key challenges, punctuated with some suspicions, hope and failure syndromes metamorphosing, family responsibilities rearing their indispensable heads, extended and nuclear, moving away from immediate household to extended household, all beginning to take hard tolls on the partners, the Postliminal which could have been the most relaxed stage, may become the more troubling stage, when, if care is not taken, partners begin to regress, fighting to win favors, mainly of their children' love, care and support. At this stage, sexual interests begin to dwindle more, among the female partners. This Postliminal stage is so delicate, because, at this period, the female partners will quietly open their Invisible Diaries, Inventories and Records being stored in their sub-unconsciousness of how best or worst they were first treated and regarded by their husbands and his relatives at their pre-marital or preliminal stage in courtship and marriage. At this stage too, nature may not pardon those stone-hearted husbands who presumably and arrogantly claimed overwhelming superiority, degraded and sold off their wives so cheap in front of their family members and friends, mishandled them for no offenses at all, except to win total control of the house, property and the marriage rank. Whether the men want it or not, at this point, women become unbeatably fierce, totally in control of the entire household, property, children and their love. This period is often referred to, as "the Supreme Regime of Women, SRW". Thus, this Guide *"ab initio"* warms all husbands to avoid any form of maltreatment on their wives, especially when they are newly married to you from a different home, environment and family backgrounds.

The care and love you show to your wife at the preliminal stage, determines how best or worst you later enjoy or live in your marriage, because, according to Jamison: "We all carry burdens with us that others don't suspect. And those burdens color how we feel and how we think… and they affect whether or not we are able to risk and grow" in our marriage (Jamison, 1989:36) or die! This very situation in marriage imperatively calls for caution.

As it were, every state in life is unique in itself. As a priest of the Most High God, despite my trials, joys, ups and downs, I am ever grateful to God, the Initiator and Owner of vocations and would want married people also to share the same joy in their own state. I do not intend to discuss the "theology of marriage" here. My earlier work on Traditional Marriage - *"Igba Nkwu Nwanyi"* has taken care of that. Do not regard this, either, as an academic publication or a dissertation as such!

All the same, marriage is life lived and celebrated! It exclusively exists between two rational principal agents who have freely agreed to live as husband and wife. It is a life shared in absolute freedom, a covenant sealed in love of God and man. In other words, every marriage is unique in itself. A traditional marriage differs from that of the Church because of variations in the forms or rites. The Church marriage is a Sacrament, pure and simple! Besides, marriage is the highest and best School of learning, where only the candidates sit, unguarded, self- solely score, grade and pass or fail themselves! That is, no marriage exists in a vacuum or by proxy.

Therefore, for a marriage to be authentic or valid, it must take place and witnessed within a particular culture, Church, milieu or society that accepts it as such, with its norms and customs. Thus, whether you call this coming together of a man and a woman, marriage, a celebration, a solemnization, a ceremonial display, a wedding etc., it is one and the same thing. And this is precisely why there cannot be any dichotomy between marriage and wedding. However, marriage being a form of mystery has its own language which only the particular couples understand. It may not necessarily require a formula or venue. The exchange of consent can be an oral affair, a simple nodding of the head, wearing of rings, handing over a cup of palm wine, depending on one's own culture. Marriage can take place on the road, at a market place, in the Church, at a funeral service, in a religious crusade. Yet, it must be within a context. The two in question provide the matter and the Church witnesses and provides the Liturgical Form of marriage. The mystery of marriage lies on the fact that it had already taken place before the public is notified. Consequently, why do we speak about "wedding without marriage today"

Surely, from the point of view of marriage itself, it is the same thing as wedding. But, judging from the practical aspect of it, most couples have sharply separated one from the other. They seem to have made nonsense of it today due to obvious reasons. In other words, cases abound where people now wed before their Community - "Umunna" or in the Church for other reasons than becoming husbands and wives. This is saliently why we had intended to have our topic read: "Wedding without marriage". Among the factors that dangerously influence some people in their choices and decisions to marriage today may include:

1. The urge to sex or physical attractions to this particular person. I ca 'lack of proper knowledge' of what marriage actually means;
2. Seeing marriage or wedding as a measure of achievements. For instanc mates have all married, why not me?
3. Wedding for economic reasons alone. I have spent so much on o weddings; I must get married to the rich and regain what I have sp them;
4. Marriage as an occasion to display ones affluence or financial status;
5. Legality to claim their spouse's property in the event of sudden death.

This, being the case, what do we say of those who simulate marriages by saying "Yes' when they inwardly mean "No" and vice versa? Some people marry through photographs. What happens when a person is photogenic in photographs but very ugly looking in manners and appearances? Nowadays, many Christians prefer traditional wedding to the Church wedding or even to live together without any marriage! What are they really afraid of? May be, to avoid being life-committed, get stuck or tired down to one partner? In a situation like this, human wisdom equals to zero before God! That is way, especially in Africa; "Trial marriage" – a practice, in which the female counterpart must first be put into the family way to prove or to assure of her fertility, is evil. Does this not look like tempting or setting traps for God? For me, to do this, is to take a big risk in one's future. Some even mess up the Christian marriage - the Sacrament of matrimony by equating and comparing it with court marriage, traditional or "Igba Nkwu Nwanyi. Some do stop half way, even after their wedding, forgetting so quickly the paraphernalia of the ceremony, the gorgeous crowd that occasioned it and shortly begin to mess up and misbehave. What of those Christians who no longer want marriage instructions at all before wedding? In fact, this is why I deemed it necessary to play the midwife to all those, whose vocations are matrimonial, mainly to assist them.

Thus, our emphasis here is centered on achieving a happy life in marriage as such. In this context therefore, traditional and Christian marriages are not mutually exclusive. Our stand point may assist all those who are directly or indirectly involved in the race. Couples need to understand why their partners behave the way they do because what a husband or wife hates in each other may be in him or her as well. Thus, I am offering married people a type of spiritual tonic. Let them meditate on it and decipher why they must have to get married or remain single. As a Guide, raptly meditate on these 50 steps to happy married life. My brother and sister in love, as you pray and work on these steps, do create space and allow the Mother of the Church and our Own Mother, Mary, to intercede for you. Amen!

Additionally, in this Marriage Guide, I have decided to apply my area of specialty in "Spiritual psychology" within the field of psychological practice, which examines issues from their futuristic long-term benefits and perspectives to guide the moment. It offers society and individuals, some behavior alert vitamins, impulse controls, inner strengths, emotional muscles, internal energies, high consciousness, positive spiritual connections, self-affirmation and strong sense of who a person is. Each couple, flexibly, needs to understand a bit of himself, trust in his nature and capacity to adapt, build, resuscitate and motivate 'the will to live' and smoothly move on with his choicest relationship. Get ready, set, and please, before taking off, go with God! Blessings!

A. PRELIMINAL STEPS TO THE JOURNEY

1. MATURITY

Maturity is strength! It is awareness of the obvious, the stability, knowledge and understanding of the self, others and environment. Partners need it to be successful in their relationships. Every marriage requires spiritual maturity and not necessarily the "physical". The ability to positively give alternative reasons to excuse the other is of paramount importance in marriage. Maturity too, covers a lot of things that could generate misgivings in marriage. Of course, frequent quarrelling in marriage is a sign of immaturity – spiritual. Maturity includes creative intelligence and humility for a partner to admit and own his limitations, growing edges, shortcomings, and the ability to learn and master when to say "Yes or No" and be open to corrections, suggestions to behave, begin afresh and do the right thing or the noted wrong thing, differently. Every human relationship requires and demands, not only the physical maturity, but also the emotional. Here lie the maturity and sole rule of marital engagement. That is, a partner's view of their marriage, even love may change with events or time, but the maturity to concretely behold the same marriage for what it really is, does not change. Maturity guides a partner to be less judgmental or quick to condemn and lose temper on his partner, especially in public! The case of Joseph, whose wife, Mary seemed to have cheated, is a big guide here. As the Christian Bible expressed it: "Before they came to live together she was found to be with child.... Her husband Joseph; being a man of honor and wanting to spare her publicity, decided to divorce her informally" (Mat. 1:18-19). Can any of our married men of today, tolerate, accept or learn anything from Joseph, especially when he was being backed up by law? I am yet to hear of such men, because of the exclusive emphasis placed on sex! This is not to support cheating in any form or shape. Marriage should not be limited to sex alone. Love covers a great multitude of sin! Therefore, criticizing and exposing your partner's weakness before an opposite sex is sheer display of immaturity and affected ignorance. On no grounds should partners indulge in such acts of fraud, breach of trust, call it nepotism which is equal to a total betrayal, if not destruction of self-image and willful deterioration of matrimonial vows! We can only imagine how such self-righteous, foolish looking; betrayer-partners might appear before their targeted accomplices or victims. Very wise partners, indeed? Why not act responsibly, appreciate your own marriage and leave others to enjoy theirs in peace, because nothing else trumps happiness and peace of mind?

Now, let us face it! Assuming that, you once, unintentionally cheated on your partner, why not sternly feel guilty of your sin, humbly amend your ways, ask for forgiveness from your God, promise yourself never to repeat it and move on, ensuring your partner, with repentant heart, of your unalloyed and deep sorrow for not listening to him as you should. The cheating might not be my worry! I feel so sorry for all of us who violate our marital and sacerdotal vows, especially when we seem to normalize and pride in them with no single remorse of any sort, at best, we tend to reassure ourselves by referring to the boundless mercy of God. For Christians, if Jesus Himself, as Peter observed: "Bore our sins in his body on the cross, that we might die to sin and live to righteousness (1 Peter 2:24), has His expiation or atonement on the cross then guaranteed our salvation, irrespective of however we live our lives now, to sin or not? I don't think so! The fact that He had already died on the cross so that "we might die to sin and live for righteousness" remains a platitude, sacrosanct, certain that God's mercy eternally goes with an inescapable judgment. Believe it or not, if I had not, early, in 1970, physically and personally witnessed and heard the voices of the spirits of the dead, marketing – shouting in their thousands around 1 or 2 am as they sell and buy in a popular old Eke Nguru market in Mbaise, Imo State, Nigeria, and being pulled backwards myself by these dead spirits without any physical touch, and left again (I mean myself) as I shouted to my companion that day, Mr. Adolphus from Itu Ezinihitte, "please wait for me", there was no way on the planet then, I would have ever believed the story if someone else had narrated same to me? A long story, but 100% true! Life is as mysterious as marriage itself! Partners must solemnly approach it with every degree of maturity, dedication and respect, period!

Consequently, the Johari window model of Joseph Luft and Harry Ingham, created in the US in 1955, can be of classic importance in every marriage. They created 4 widow models to represent a cognitive psychological tool or skill that can help individuals or partners especially in corporate settings to understand one another better for smoother relationships. The said window is in a form of a house with 4 rooms, in which each room refers or contains individual qualities, values or vital pieces of information that assist each individual or partner to self-supervise him or herself. For instance, while two rooms have information that is accessible to others, the contents of the other two rooms are unknown to others. The first room represents part of our life patterns or values that others know about us and we know them too. The second room specifies those qualities (blind spot quadrants) of ours, which are only known by others but unknown to us. This is where partners are called to deeply reflect upon, for which each may be misjudged by the other, and vice versa. By implication, this is the very room that creates conflicts in marriages, because, some partners may not like to be blamed or hear anything about their ugly sides or stories. While the third room points to our unconscious or subconscious selves, which mysteriously remain unknown, both to us and others, the fourth room represents our private lives we know very well about, and keep only to ourselves (IR). Honesty and acknowledgments of one's mistakes in marriage are huge signs of maturity, which are both therapeutic and medicinal.

2. LOVE

This 4-lettered word "Love" is the controlling power, the binding force and life wire of marriage! It is the spiritual foundation upon which marriage covenant is solidified. It must be visible! Here, sincerity and openness are unquestionably irreplaceable. Love does not require any costing or coating! Love everybody but relate with few! Therefore, couples should see this love as a cross, sacrificial and sympathetic. For, dependency is not love. It is a natural antidote to any chaotic circumstance in all relationships. It is effervescent, sparking, vivacious and spiritedly fiery! Love is never enveloped or canned! At times, it sleeps in the same bed with hatred, with specific tones of language. To relate well in marriage, each partner must speak the language of love, treat each other as valid, recognize and appreciate the little efforts each makes for each other. The emotion that led two individuals to marriage at first should be respected, daily re-enacted and allowed to fan that union. We teach and tell others how to treat, love and relate with us. To love, one must fix one's shoes first! That is, each partner must examine his inabilities, weaknesses and humbly admit their presence, then work on them to cope with the reasonable and acceptable norms and mannerisms of marriage in a given culture. Each should, passionately avoid hurting the other by putting on the correct and relational attires that smell 'love welcome o o o!' When couples economize on their love for each other, they simply succeed in covering their hearts but not their bodies as "I want you" is not the same thing as "I love you," because, openness and sincerity of heart are two irreplaceable ingredients of love. In love, partners grow in each other and cover his or her back!

On a different but related note, women should be encouraged to dress decently, especially the way they feel fit, but not, in doing so, delay important appointments, like social and religious functions! Research has shown that women take longer time to comfortably dress up and apply some make ups. Men should note that! They do so, not necessarily to please anybody - their husbands or friends. Each woman dresses as her spirit moves her! Their husbands must oblige them! Worthy of note, includes the fact that women, despite their unlimited nature to care, show incomparable love to their families, particularly to their partners, they can also be the deadliest groups of human beings on the planet once they have exhausted their endurance and patience or unnecessarily pushed to the wall. Our male spouses please take note! On no condition should husbands misinterpret their wives' ever readiness and dispositions to show their love, as feeble-mindedness or weakness on their part. Never! Of course, when partners begin to mount flimsy excuses or reasons upon reasons, to avoid staying together, either in sexual matters or other serious discussions, except in obvious and understandable cases as sickness, tiredness from strenuous works, so busy to complete urgent assignments, they unforeseeably create a costly and regrettable red flag in their relationship.

Again, love in marriage is a shared identity of joy, peace and frustrations, sorrow, loss and gain, etc. Partners should freely and willingly embrace the positive and negative qualities of each other. In support of the above views, Johann observes: "When love is interested, when the attraction is based on a motive of profit or need, it has no difficulty in finding words to justify it. When "I love you" equals "I want you," the expected satisfaction of the want is reason enough for the love (1966:19). Sad indeed, because, anything that threatens any marriage, equally affects each member of that family in a very drastic - dramatic way. For a partner to tempt; stage or set a trap for the other as the best way to prove his love is, not only diabolical, satanic, but also childish. That was precisely the point James once made: "Everyone who knows the right thing to do and does not do it commits a sin" (Jam. 4:17). As noted already, a partner should never perceive his partner's friendly gesture with any form of discomfort. If you love her, then show it! Love is never pretentious! Dr. Wayne W. Dyer, in one of his TV Shows, rightly noted: "When your cup of relationship is full, stop pouring". Partners be very careful!

Besides, it is crucial to observe here that love and sex are two different values. Profound love can still exist without sex. Generally, while sex can be an expression of romantic (eros) or philia love, most often, it is not equivalent to marital love. Physically, humans share erotic love or sex along with other living beings or creatures. Philia love, according to Kant, in Nwachukwu (1993:10) "is pathological in the sense that it is based on affection and attraction", which is vital in marriage. But what happens to love when those physical attractions fade? It is also described, as 'unitive' love in married state. Again, the Christian aspects of love, "agape," the "virginal and appreciative", are values, shared by both the rational and the supernatural beings. This is where love goes beyond physical bounds and makes the love in marriage more meaningful. That was the love Paul recommended when he said: "It does not dishonor others, it is not self-seeking, it is not easily angered, it keeps no record of wrongs (1Cor. 13:5). To this effect, partners must desist from displaying their love primarily to mock those who are seriously in pain or trouble.

3. FAITH

As a supernatural gift of God, faith is self conviction, and hopefully guides couples to successful results and makes them unshakable at all cross roads of life. Only faith guarantees the objective for which marriage exists and leads to decision making. No one should underestimate the vintage and ageless role of faith in any state of life, because *Nemo dat quod non habet* – no one gives what he hasn't. To have faith is to believe in what one values, cherishes and appreciates, that may go beyond physical calculations. According to Pope Francis, "To live by faith means to put our lives in the hands of God, especially in our most difficult moments". Partners, who believe in each other, easily understand, forgive, move on, ignore their mistakes and reinforce the little efforts they make, because faith in God or marriage only works in perseverance and truth.

4. CHOICE

This is fundamental in marriage! It is a stepping stone to happy marriage, exercised in absolute freedom. Basing one's choice on the physical features alone may be risky. For instance, if the focal point in making the choice is sex, what happens when a partner falls sick or gets old? This is when prayers play vital roles! More importantly, everybody should have reasons for getting married or to be married in the first place, even to remain single or for choosing religious lives. The choices we make in life help to shape the type of personality partners invariably become in their marriage. The term "type", identifies a certain collection of traits "characteristic pattern of behavior or conscious motive which can be self-assessed or assessed by peers that make up a broad, general personality classification" (Sonderegger,1998:124) in relationships. It is natural! To behave "true to type" emotionally and culturally makes a world of difference in human interactions, behaviors, opinions, particularly, in the ways partners understand, perceive and relate to each other. Besides all the odds and ends in marriage, partners should always channel their strengths, goals, dreams, potentials and deliberations on choices that are in agreement with their set goals and resources. After all, the choices we make of things, often, do not change their reality on the ground. For instance, that family 'A" wants to own a big house does not mean she can have it. Don't be envious of other peoples' lots, manage yours! In choosing a life partner, therefore, one needs to understand some of the paradoxical antitheses in human nature that a slim or heavy girl being married today may grow bigger or slimmer tomorrow, respectively. Married men should be ready to contend with such inevitable package of life and gladly stick to their earlier or fundamental options.

5. PRAYER

Prayer is the language of heaven, an engagement with God. It is an admission of God's presence, refusal to doubt and belief in faith, that the 'needs' sought in prayer are already granted. Prayer could be an expression of one's humble self which could be a thanksgiving, ones deplorable situations, a plea and hope for the best before a superior. A heart-felt prayer plays a magical role between heaven and earth, between God and man! Always pray that your Creator, destiny, may love, protect and bless your ways. Prayer changes and transforms lives, uplifts and inspires rightful decisions, meaningful choices and unites actions. Prayer is essentially unity, leading to internal joy and peace, because nothing on the planet can be more powerful than God. No partner or person can succeed in this one single life without prayers. Prayer is an earthly way of life, a deed or conversation, eternally processed, rated and scored. Answers to our prayers always come in surprised vessels! A prayer point can also center on your partner, to maintain and cultivate the right spirit that can assist two of you enjoy your marriage. Praying that God may punish your enemies is indirectly to assume God's position. Leave Him alone! He is not a baby! Partners should simply and reasonably do what they are supposed to do and pointlessly stop creating extra and more work for God! Prayer rather lubricates marriage problems and moves those who hate us to repentance. Of course, 'prayer-less' couples are as good as dead brutes. As we face endless battles and challenges in our personal lives, prayer is a must. Therefore, couples should invite and talk to God in whatever steps they take in their marriage because prayers also hide most of the obnoxious human elements that could cause frictions in their marriages and families. Do yourself that favor and pray often!

6. GOD

God has a plan for each us as the Proprietor and Designer of relationship/marriage. The "All Knowing God" should not be taken for granted, by surprise or mystified by any single partner. Man being a "*homo religiousus*", awakes and arrivals at the early morning of religious consciousness at maturity in his super ego. According to the Koran perspective, religion is natural to everybody. For children, most often, their parents determine for them which one they belong. Hence, Massignon in Zundel maintains that "God is not an invention, he is a discovery" (1993:26). We can only discover and experience Him through sound moral life. Unlike God, human beings are invented and created by God Himself; only few partners realize this favor, discover and appreciate Him in their marriage. He does not lack, go wrong or make mistakes! This is precisely, why marriage is a free gift of God's Hypostatic union in the Blessed Trinity. The way each partner appreciates, manages and uses it, remains his own blessing or curse. Amazingly, Oprah Winfrey, in one of her TV shows, remarked: "Everything is in divine order, like it or not" (12/11/09). He has already made Himself available to us, either we cooperate with Him or go our own ways. At the end, the ultimate prize of our choices is on our heads – peace on earth and eternal life with Him or self-deceit and eternal damnation! Thus, once couples reserve a place for God in their lives and homes, call on Him in times of joy and need, the issue of fears in their marriage will surely vanish. He is always a friend of silence and not noise, because in noise, we tend to hear ourselves but in silence we hear Him. In any state of life, especially in marriage, priestly or religious, always and wholeheartedly entrust yourself in your Creator's care and go with Him, both in your decisions and actions. For, any concerns, petitions and conditions placed in God's hands never get damaged, lost or rotten. Stop complaining and worrying! These demoralizing factors have no place in the divine equation. Instead, trust all your worries to Him and remain positive in your struggles! That is why some prayers seem to be insults on God, especially when the supplicants have no remorse for their bad life styles and habits. Partners need to establish personal covenant with God as their everyday GPS system, as He regards and treats each of us as His only child, to assist them navigate their marital journey of life, particularly, towards the road to integrity, learning moral probity, hard work, peace, hope, joy and love. At times, they may misinterpret their GPS due to wordily distractions, make mistakes, follow wrong directions; yet, it does not blame or abandon them on the way. With confidence, if they listen more carefully and pay attention to each other, it automatically reconnects them on the right path to their set objectives. Believe it or not, whatever God permits or allows is good, because He runs the show!

7. THE CHURCH

The Church – the people of God is eternally founded on rock. She is a beacon guiding all Christian marriages, providing them with the Word of God and the Sacraments. Hence, Pope Francis, the man of his word, in his *"Gaudete Exsultate"* – 'rejoice and be glad', calls each person to holiness in the small kind gestures rendered to others. A good family, being the domestic Church, draws its living water from the Church. Those who strongly identify with Her, not only enjoy their relationships on earth but also ensure their lives with eternity in heaven. Through the Church, partners will be able to see the face of Christ, (humility exemplified) in each other, so as to slow down in rash decisions and behave. The family is the domestic Church only when she has proved and made herself worthy of being one. That is why society can *ipso facto* worship God better with more industries around her, than the building of churches and prayer houses among hungry people! While the Church may, through her Sacraments and teachings prepare, encourage, witness and declare young men and women as husbands and wives, She does not force, dictate, monitor or recommend them to a particular marriage. Marriage is exclusively between the man and woman! The couple invites the Church, period!

8. TRUST

It is of ranking importance for couples to trust themselves in marriage. Once suspicion sets in at any point, trouble must certainly explode. To ensure a happy home, couples must have to use only one eye or at best, entirely close their four eyes on their mistakes. This does not remove the place of misunderstanding in marriage. But, 1 believe, misunderstanding can be a timely warning for couples to take the right steps in their lives. In this sense, a husband should not expect his wife to be honest and caring when he is greedy and selfish. Or, is it possible for partners to steal from each other or become thieves themselves by their 'hide and seek' attitudes? Obviously, whenever suspicion sets in or occurs in a marriage, partners begin to hide certain information from each other, thereby robbing themselves, others, including their own offspring, (if they have any), of those moral values and basics that generally harmonize relationships and lives, because when one finger gets soiled, it may eventually infect the rest. Believe it or not, there is no miracle or magic in a marriage the partners are careless about or not prepared, ready to maintain and keep. Sound moral lives are the engines, keys, the partners' internal energy, system memories, and power manifestations of healthy marriages. On no condition should any partner be taken as a spare part supplier of needs, a piece of furniture he or she can replace at will for any reasons whatsoever! Never should a partner be considered as an object under a shoe, that can freely be removed once he pulls off his feet from it or an 'agency theory' where a third party has to be delegated. For instance, for a husband to cheat on his wife, pick quarrels with her when she is pregnant or nursing a baby is conceitedly the highest form of psychotic display, insensibility and idiocy as well. Marriage, being the two sides of a coin, is not an hourly or monthly affair. It is life, confidently lived in total trust, sacrifice and love! It takes only one partner to ensure peace and unity in a marriage or set it ablaze. Thus, as human feelings have no banks of their own; partners must express them to each other, either peacefully or confrontationally. Note well: "No partner is an island in any marriage!" Marriage is 'two separate lives' cemented in trust.

B. THE LIMINALITY OF THE JOURNEY

9. WEDDING

Ritually, wedding is a mark of identity in a particular culture, be it traditional or Christian. It does not, as a ceremony today, necessarily add much to the life that is marriage itself. For instance, in traditional wedding, couples exchange a cup of palm wine, while in the Christian perspective, rings. Therefore, couples should try to fan their marriages into deeper love by reenacting, reliving and making anew the same old wedding ceremony every day. They can do this periodically, now, using water for palm wine and handshakes for rings. Let couples try to be funny at times or foolish to allow peace reign in their families. The ceremony may add nothing to the Sacrament that is being solemnized, if the partners have not made up their minds and entrusted their commitment to God and destiny. While the world may have gathered to rejoice with and show their solidarity and support with the partners, only they, themselves, decide where they go and what to do after their supporters have all taken their leave? Either, to first kneel down, thank God for their good friends or to start wondering how much money they made? Any marriage tied up with money, is often, likely or eventually going to fail. Be careful! We make a living with what we can get or afford, but life with what we can give out or share with others!

10. THE SELF

Marriage is a combination of two opposite selves, which naturally may be opposed to each other in degree and function. Yet, in marriage, the two must have to agree. Expecting so much comfort from marriage is dangerous. Couples can present false selves to themselves. It is natural and unavoidable! But, I am pleading that couples destroy part of their former selfish selves and make little efforts to accommodate or marry only what is necessary for the married life. For, no man or woman can completely be mastered. The 'self or personal story" is the foundation upon which a successful or unsuccessful marriage is anchored. In their own words, Capuzzi & Gross observed: "The manners in which people think and feel affect their lives" (2003:214). The situation becomes troubling and pitiable when a partner or pastor who needs substantial help in marriage or ministry, always claims to be right in his decisions, choices and actions. No wonder, Norman, within the principles of cognitive-behavioral therapy, stated: "Physicians have long known that a patient who expects to get pain relief from a pill often does (foolishly as it were), even though it is a placebo containing no medication" (Norman, 2007:191). Self-consciousness guides every partner to expect the unexpected in his or her marriage, even when the atmosphere in their family sounds friendly and welcoming, simply because individual stories differ. Every partner needs a survival personality inside him or her, despite the inevitable storms and exigencies of life, that might most often, than anticipated, gradually unfold in their marriage. You can self-reflectively contend with and smoothly handle them. To this end, pay heed to Jamison in these words: "You do have power. Yes you do. It comes from the very center of yourself-your kernel-the part of you that is unique" (1989:43) and nobody else gives it to you. Partners must, hitherto, set their own life standards and patiently work on them. In achieving this goal, they must tell themselves the simple truth, have strong sense of who they are; morally do the best they can and ignore some of the living standards, others have set for their own families. Partners deserve the best in their marriage, period!

Believe it or not, our Stories differ. Always try and give your relationship a name that identifies your feelings and values. While the faces of human relationships may differ, each individual is unique. Donze T. Mary once said: "You are the only one person like you that makes you special. And because everyone else is just himself or herself and nobody else, that makes everyone else special, too, but each in a different way" (1998:70). The fact is that, every relationship is shaped by its own story. Every family should shape her own story, necessarily because our individual identities, personalities and stories differ. Thus, we are both our stories and values! Our lives are perceived as stories, and every name or marriage is associated with a particular story. As Crites Steven has insightfully observed in Rabbi Goldberg and Jay: "A man's sense of his own identity seems largely determined by the kind of story which he understands himself to have been enacting through…the story of his life (1983:13). That is to say, in as much as our stories and values are different, partners cannot be expected to behave exactly the same way in certain circumstances. This is what constitutes major obstacles in most marriages. Partners, as a matter of fact, need to underline this point. It has been medically proved that each person's heart is distinctive from the other, scientifically speaking and "no two hearts are the same". Yet, the three layers of the heart perform the same functions, beautifully and harmoniously working together to keep us alive! Eventually, in every healthy marriage, the partners should work together and pay less attention on who gets the credit and focus on their joint benefits. Just as the whole parts of our body are different but work together to keep us alive, every family should also relate as human beings, and benefit from their socio-cultural diversities and enjoy the uniqueness of each other.

11. HUSBAND AND WIFE

These are the principal agents of marriage, the two singular big elephants on the celestial race! They are the living organisms of every family with heads and parts. The husband is the head (the central, unifying system) of the family, while the wife represents the various parts (distracting and unifying). Since none of them can operate without the other, the two must oscillate to bring the desired balance, peace, unity and progress. They have to work along with each other in love and harmony and with one mind; they can easily cross the boundaries of their differences, always acknowledging and listening to each other's feelings. The partners are the symbol and representative of the face of the members of God's family, the Church. Husband and wife are not only the domestic Church, but the microcosm of society. That is meaningfully why the partners should not just mess up their union because of personal gains or selfishness and expect to go scot free from God's bitter judgment. While it is naturally and divinely endorsed that a man and woman live together as husband and wife, it is better to be alone than die in toxic relationship or marriage, vows notwithstanding. Why not/*Anukwa M akuko!* No wonder some refuse to marry, just to enjoy their privacy and independence!

12. LIVING TOGETHER

Things are hard, no doubts. In other words, one of the couples may leave the house in pursuit of employment somewhere else. This is normally welcomed, but not recommended! It becomes detestable and evil when one of them stays away from the other for years. Consult the Exodus 32:1 case: "If the people Moses was leading himself, even to the cost of his own life, apostatized simply because he delayed coming down from the mountain, just for their own good, and forced Aaron to make gods for them with their own ear rings and necklaces, the partner who keeps away, so long, from his home may be propagating infidelity. Therefore, my advice is that couples should try and live together! This life commitment – 'living together' also entails serious disagreements because of ignorance of the basic fact on the ground and whose solutions they can supply too. In this case, when it is impossible, let them agree to meet occasionally, the side effects notwithstanding. As already noted, every marriage speaks its own language. It is not hard to learn– live and let the other live also! Thus, language, being a powerful means of communication, cannot be underestimated in all interpersonal relationships. Emotional language may distinctively convey a journey of no specific destination, but can easily be understood by every sincere player in the game. Living together can be hell or a fun once partners freely and gladly share their ups and downs together! For me, marriage is not necessarily about the other partner, but the knowledge of myself as a team player, as to avoid hurting my partner. While I may not effectively control the actions of my partner, my honest efforts to set the pace and shape the nature of our relationship, may lead to an agreeable moment where my partner may freely, joyously and always comply with me. Living together begins with and ends with you/me! As Henry Home in Mead F. would have it: "The difficulty is not so great to die for a friend, as to find a friend worth dying for" (1965:156). No wonder then, Lauder Robert noted: "Friendship is the greatest gift: in it, what is given is the self" (1978:72). Elaborating more on the nature of a "gift", he added: "What makes a gift so attractive is that the giver is not compelled to give it... Gifts are signs of the giver. That's probably why often it is difficult to pick a gift. The more special the person who will receive it is, the more difficult the giver's task in choosing the gift" (Ibid, 1978:72) becomes. Partners are just gifts to themselves and society, if they cooperate! As for that man or woman who has married more than once, may be, in his or her 4th relationship now, and yet encounters problems there, should deeply examine him or herself, because the root cause of the breakups must be within! For instance, the mismanagement of the economy of any society or family has never been traced to the spirit world, but to us, humans! The English Philosopher, Thomas Hobbes did say it: "*Homo est homini lupus* – Man is a wolf to man." By 'man' here, he was not even referring to a friend or relation, but to a possible life partner whom one has not seen or met before, a stranger. Thus, most partners were once strangers, a fact that calls for serious study and learning. Be careful!

Accordingly, partners direly need each other to create devotional space for themselves, live and enjoy their marriage. As it were, to exist in a relationship is not the same thing as to live, because marriage is an organic identity, progressive and proactive. It is a full time ministry, a Sacrament! Partners should give themselves personal life-endearing and fulfilling names that can always remind and challenge them to maintain their marriage equilibrium. The life of grace is indeed a challenge because to achieve excellence in marriage or any field in human life is not by chance. Partners have to work for it! They merely exist when there is no peace, truth or justice, but live when there is unruffled and unperturbed state of mind, that is encompassed in deep sense of identity and belongingness. Partners need to know that there may not be any perfect or total trustworthy husband or wife on the planet. Hold firm and cherish the one you have! Even the most joyous marriage can, at times, be both peaceful and chaotic, without any affect on the marriage bond. Let the partners optimistically keep struggling together, aiming to remain the centers of admirations and good examples among colleagues. This is vital because the only worse thing in marriage is when a particular partner, being accused or regarded as a bad one or a cheat proves the accusation to be true by his actions. In Fulton Sheen's own words: "Peace means a right conscience, not a dictatorship over the proletariat…not the overthrow of society; it means loving our enemies, not despising them; it means something in the inside of a man's soul, not something outside like a sickle and a hammer" (1989:221-222). Each partner must embody peace, joy and the world around them in his marriage. Paths to peace do not necessarily count on the details of the wrong behaviors of a partner, because, in peace, the mind only recollects positive memories that energize progress. There is peace when we choose well, work hard, shape our destinies, priorities and plan within our reach. Partners must allow each other to be and live his or her life. No wonder then, Hawkins David wrote: "It is a relief to let the mind become silent and just 'be' with the surroundings. Peace results, and appreciation and calm prevail…. The well-disciplined mind should only speak when requested to perform a task" (2006:234). For instance, you cannot expect your partner to smile, dance or feel at home with you when you deliberately avoided or failed to listen to his or her concerns. For the sake of peace, whenever your partner tells you: "Stop", please, calmly confirm it and say: "I am sorry" till you get a response. Singular heartfelt gestures of open-mindedness and sincerity are highly rewarded and reciprocated in a variety of ways in healthy relationships, particularly when partners understand themselves and their limitations. This peace is not eternal, always guaranteed in many marriages because of the unpredictability of life which no one has control over. Just as relationships are not presumptuous, there might never be a neutrality or perfection in them due to the uniqueness of each partner. For instance, amidst love, joy, progress and peace, hatred, sadness, failure and quarrel co-exit. Prudence is essential here! Partners must not allow the memories of negative past events or failures to frustrate and determine their present status. It is better they focus on their positive life styles, little achievements, memories which are vital ingredients of life that motivate fruitful accomplishments. Keep on doing good and let nature take its course, because happy is the partner or person who is contented with the little or least he has. Here, happiness is not getting whatever you want at all times, but loving and cherishing the little you already have! On this, I remind partners to take note that 'music' is divine and boundless! It hears all languages and has no enemies. Thus, they must always appreciate each other to enjoy his or her taste and brand of music, period! You can just complement his or her choice for peace!

13. SELF-CONTROL

Man is a bundle of possibilities. The ability for a partner to manage, control his emotions and actions, especially when provoked by his partner and re-adjust his feelings to an unfriendly or irritating stimulus for the sake of God and peace is encouraged in marriage. Therefore, couples should try and perform only those actions that are in alignment with their state. For, marriage attains its maximum degree of success in self-control. It is an embodiment and encapsulation of ideas, virtues, graces and vices too, depending on how each partner handles them. Naturally, for instance, a partner may easily get angry, especially when the good behavior or response he expects from his partner is not there or exhibited. Yes, that is normal, but discretion and patience strongly count here, too! Oblige me to add: "First and foremost, partners should control their anger and NEVER, ever make arbitrary decisions or act on them, that is, in extreme anger, even when they are backed up by all the reasons in the world to be so". Experiences have also shown that in anger, a partner can easily bite the finger that feeds him. Also, partners should avoid texting, phone calls, voice messaging or writing each other, vent or aggressively transfer their workplace toxic experiences or someone's headache or *'palava'* down to their family or partner in anger. If you cannot deal with it there, then forget it, unless your partner needs to know about it. In such a case, you can only present the ugly incident at that workplace as a matter of concern, where you indirectly seek for compassion from your partner! No one doubts that anger is positive and necessary at times! Every human being needs it, because through anger, partners genuinely and reasonably open their hearts and register their grievances against each other that call for immediate attention. However, if anger is not controlled, it can create unredeemable consequences. Each partner should calmly examine why his partner angrily talked or behaved that way to him and humbly and regretfully acknowledge the anger and invite her for a friendly talk.

At this point, there is every need to study the role ego defense mechanisms play, particularly in marriage. So many Psychotherapists, Psychiatrists and Psychologists like Sigmund Freud, Erik Erikson, Morgan, John H, Sonderegger & Romero and Kemp and Hilgard and Atkinson, just to mention a few, have extensively studied human behaviors and have directly and indirectly, come up with practically-oriented ways by which single individuals and married ones could blamelessly relate and enjoy their lives. Partners need to understand the falsehood of defense mechanism (DM) and consciously avoid getting involved with such unconscious behaviors that might hamper trust and confidence in their relationships. This observation is so important because in DM, most partners arrogantly and ignorantly, even at times, surreptitiously and secretively live false selves in their marriage. Such partners, chiefly the male ones unconsciously operate on their animalistic psyche, the "id", thereby, acting like babies, unsympathetically seek immediate self gratifications and pleasures. We regard such partners as the "IF" of marriage, meaning, the "I, First" Syndromes in whatever they say or do! Thus, they create major problems in their relationships. Partners must note that reliable and trustworthy relationships are explicitly basic to human lives. For instance, John Powell in his book entitled "Why am I afraid to tell you who I am?" expressed it better in these words: "Person is resonant (full-bodied) to person.... If I am willing to step out of the darkness of my prison, to expose the deepest part of me to another person, the result is almost always automatic and immediate: The other person feels empowered to reveal himself to me. Having heard of my secret and deep feelings, he is given the courage to communicate his own. This, in the last analysis, is what we mean by 'encounter" or [relationship - mine] (1969:85). The inability of any partner to smoothly relate and interact with the other is cancerous and deadly. Hence, Hilgard and Atkinson noted that: "The chief characteristic of the antisocial personality is a lack of moral development or conscience, and an inability to abide by the laws and customs of his society" (1967:541). Psychotics should not be allowed to marry or function as Pastors of any Church till they get the professional help they urgently need. Prospective partners, their parents and our Church Leaders need to know this, that before some individuals step into marriage or being assigned Parishes as Pastors, respectively, they must be fully prepared. For instance, according to Dr. Alexis Carrel, in one of his masterpieces, "Man the Unknown" observed that every normal human being has some percentage of madness". If this is the case, then, what happens when a person, lay, priest or religious camouflages him or herself as representing the mission he or she has not properly prepared for? The bother line is: 'Most of us need psychological examinations, certified by professionals before getting into marriage or priestly ministry, let alone be appointed a Pastor or to teach in a major Seminary, period!' That swas why, Dr. A. Carrel in addressing each of us, insisted that: "You have in your head right now, 12,000,000,000, yes, twelve billion brain cells. And in every one of these brain cells, there is ongoing, continually that agitation of small particles around the nucleus in the center" (1935:17). This is revealing! These brain cells, irrespective of their number, which are continually in agitation, equally reflect in our moods, decisions, actions and they create problems in our relationships. It is easy to surmise who these psychotics are! For instance, any person, partner or religious who is consciously money and sex-oriented, focused can easily push the Gospel boat of eternal life to sink unperturbed. We can hide these inclinations from others but not from God!

Imperatively, we are constrained to deeply re-visit these defense mechanisms – DM, in order to arm partners with helpful-life saving weapons to defend what is needed in their marriage and avoid the unessential. For instance, when a partner's heart is focused on someone else, there is no point for him to pretend and make his wife believe or feel that she is the most cherished woman on the planet. This is what we refer to, as *intellectualization or isolation*. Again, where a partner unconsciously seems to displace the anger someone else caused him outside his home, only to vent or redirect his hurt to his innocent family at home, so as to affirm his lost superiority, we term it *aggressiveness or displacement*. *Evasion* is where a partner dodges his reasonable course of action or responsibility in the house with self-excuses or exoneration. It is perceived, not only as a sign of inadequacy but also immaturity. This is of 2 types; 1. *Repression*, here a partner unwillingly refuses to bring up in their discussions or keep hiding his face against any disgraceful action he must have committed in the past ; 2. In *Projection,* sometimes, a partner will protect himself from blames by comparing his undesirable qualities or weaknesses in the house with others. Most often, he assigns those weak points in an exaggerated degree to others. For instance, he feels protected whenever he says: "I may be hot-tempered or a bad husband, but so, so and so persons are the worst". Such unconscious defenses are not necessary in marriage! Partners should always and squarely deal and face their responsibilities and failures together. In a situation, where a partner wants to appear dignified in his marriage, especially, when faced with difficult and challenging moments, (especially, at postliminal stage of marriage) he begins to revert to those past joyous moments and assigns logical and positive reasons to his present actions, to avoid blames or being accused of any failures. This is regarded as *Regression*.

We still have *Substitution* - where a partner can easily proffer a solution to tough problems he has no idea of solving, instead of being honest about them and seek help. Substitution can take the form of *sublimation, compensation or overcompensation,* which is a situation where a partner may simply look like a very religious, soft-spoken person, as a philanthropist of note, especially in sexual matters, as a cover-up to those behaviors that are unacceptable by his partner or where he appears to excel in certain areas he knows he has virtually failed to achieve the desired goals, respectively. *Identification/Introjection* – is a situation where a lazy partner seems to derive his joys or sorrows by listening to wealthy peoples' stories, and often, tends to appear important by joining and spending more of his time in their company. *Fantasy* is a scenario where a partner who seems to have failed his family, relaxes by imagining of his past achievements instead of being humble enough to face the present harsh reality. *Denial* – is when a lazy partner refuses to perceive the problems of his family but pretends as if everything is normal. *Undoing* - happens more with male partners, where they try to cover up their suspicious behaviors or habits by presenting excusable reasons. For instance, a male partner who lavishes his high salary on drunkenness or other useless associations will constantly be complaining to his family of how the bad government and economy have reduced the value of money. *Doubt* – is another form of self-deception or defense mechanism where a partner seems to be playing on the intelligence of his family. For instance, Mr. Wow knew that his wife would be waiting for him to collect some money for purchases that day, and being a stingy husband, delays returning home, but calls the wife to inform her (though on his way) how busy the office work was, coupled with heavy traffic. Unpredictably, by keeping his wife in suspense, relaxes as a caring husband, not minding what happens with her going for the shopping. *Reaction formation* – is a situation, where a partner tries to hide his bad habits by endorsing the right thing to do, and using them to forge on with his trick. For instance, an alcoholic partner will always try to initiate conversations with his family on why much drinking is bad and the efforts he has made to quit drinking completely. In this case, his ego to enjoy drinking uninterruptedly agrees or resolves with his carnal self, the id – the one way traffic (his inability) to quit, yet with full knowledge and awareness of his superego (the conscience version of his judgment) that drinking can create health hazards and eventually ruin his marriage (Cf. Romero & Kemp in Nwachukwu, 2011:320).

However, before we delve into personality types and temperaments, may we briefly examine human personality structures, though noted earlier (unknown to some partners) – the 'id, ego and superego'. They affect and influence every marriage? The id is equal to youths of this present age – but very dangerous and troubling. At this infancy stage of marriage, all hands must be on deck to monitor and control the goings! It is very hard to find solutions to any human problem, especially in marriage that neglects sound moral principles. The ego, as a reality principle, is man in his real self and nature, representing his views of his environments, social realities, conscious beliefs, and the cause of his behaviors and treatments on other people et cetera. Each partner is hereby called to delay the impulses from his id first, objectively examine his proposals, decisions and humbly listen to her partner before carrying them out. It was within this context that Ekeagba noted that: "Some people describe the ego as the voice of God" (1994:6). Also, in his own words, Sigmund Freud said: "The id, a reservoir of unconscious psychic energy, operating on the pleasure principle, seeks immediate gratification, and is not restrained by reality. ...The ego, which develops in early childhood, operates through the reality principle, which seeks to gratify impulses of the id realistically and to bring long-term pleasure without pain.

The ego operates at both the conscious and pre-conscious levels. The superego, being the last of the structures to develop, begins from the age of 4 to 5 years. This is the internal representation of the traditional values, morals and norms of society as interpreted to the child by the parents and teachers at school. The superego acts as the voice of conscience and operates mostly at the preconscious level of awareness. People also possess and are driven by a psychological energy called the libido" [sex drive –mine] (Ibid.). Hence, as noted in these three structures, some full-grown partners still operate on the level or structure of the selfish 'id' in their marriage. Thereby, they unconsciously overturn the basics of sacred marriage into a total fiasco or disaster. And worst still, if such a partner had been fixated at his childhood, even as an adolescent stage of his personality development without proper resolution, he can be very rich, intelligent, an important figure in society, but will always behave as an adolescent of 11 to 14 years old in his interpersonal relationship or marriage for life. Alas! Nothing can hugely be done about it now! This is where labored attention and understanding is paramount in a marriage. The more mature partner has to patiently pet her partner to avoid fighting! Fixation takes a dangerous turn in marriage when it occurred at the phallic stage of 3 to 6 years of a partner's personality or psychosexual (libido) development, when his attention seems to center on his genitalia or sex organs. This process creates an *"Oedipus complex"* in Sonderegger's words: "Where the male child develops jealousy toward his father for competing and commanding his mother's attention or an *"Electra complex"* in which the female child or girl appears to compete with her mother for her father's love and attention. The children can easily resolve these conflicts when they identify with the parent of the same gender" *(1998:122)*. Partners need to note that, this stage is so delicate in the life of their children, especially regarding how they feel about parents. It is only with time, that such feelings will later be transferred to the outside world. For instance, a girl whose love for her father is so strong hardly stay or last in marital state. Parents must work day-in and day-out to learn how to deal with this situation, because the foundation of the future of their children's heterosexual relationships and sex orientations are heavily laid here. And those partners who show equal cares to their children are, accordingly, reciprocated.

As it were, partners should take time and study the role their 'personality types and temperaments' could play in their marriage, before they officially get married. Is this 'take time and study' not what our young boys and girls call "Dating?" Urban Dictionary sees it as: "Where two people who are attracted to each other spend time together to see if they can stand to be around each other most of the time". For me, the expression: "Most of the time….spend time together" is troubling, because the stress can be misunderstood. Why 'Most of the time and spending time' and doing what? As a Catholic clergy and minister, I am daily around my parishioners, Patients and Families, spending time with them, with fellow priests, religious and individuals at Diocesan meetings, administration of the Sacraments, in the Church, office works, home visitations for the Sick and Home bound etc. In these mutual relationships, I listen to their concerns, counsel, learn from them and enjoy their memberships myself as one God's family. Here, there are no sexual interactions. Thus, by 'dating' as expressed in that Dictionary is not a period for indiscipline, having sex or promiscuous behaviors. This is why parental sex education is vital before their kids wrongly learn or perceive it from their peers!

To put the records right, Romero and Kemp observed that: "Personality is the tendency to behave, think, and feel consistently over time and across situations" (2007:87). It is the characteristic behavior of an individual or a partner, which exactly shows the way he feels and acts. In other words, a partner's character - the big elephant in the room of relationship, is the boss that controls, builds, shapes, determines or destroys his personality in that marriage. Our actions save or ruin us! Along the same line, Tim LaHaye observed: "Temperament sets broad guidelines on everyone's behavior-pattern that influences a person as long as he lives.... The primary advantage of learning about these four basic temperaments is to discover your most pronounced strengths and weaknesses" (1988:22). Wow! Beloved Partners, this awareness is very important for you and your healthy marriage! Study yourself first before blaming others or your partner and listen to Agwulonu Fidelis, thus: "Temperament is the combination of genes and chromosomes of our parents and grandparents at conception. Temperament is not the only influence upon our behavior. ...prenatal, postnatal... influences are there to make us what we are, especially, in training, education, and motivation. Temperament, however, is the primary influence on a person's life, not because, it is the first thing that affects us, but because like body structure, color of eyes and other physical characteristics, it escorts us through life" (2001:73). Every partner has a temperament that influences and reflects in his marriage because each person is her own temperament. Temperaments are our inborn personality traits and characteristics. Partners easily tend to get along when they are conscious of each other's temperaments because they reveal our strengths, weaknesses and growing edges. Naturally, they are the ways we are and nothing can easily be done to change them. That is why as noted already, once a partner is cognizant of his temperament and that of his partner; the application of management techniques and strategies is constantly there to grace his marriage. In this way, the basic question a partner should always ask is: "What is my partner's personality type and temperament, assuming you know yours?"

Let us briefly study some of these personality types, according to Ekeagba, and how they, also, influence marriages and relationships in general. They include; (i). A *general or psychopathic* personality which refers to the emotionally immature people or partners! They hardly tell an offender his faults in his face. In any marriage where one of the partners is immature, the mature one should go extra miles to put up with certain inconveniences and difficulties in order to move the relationship forward. (ii). Just as the name suggests, *a timid* personality always fears to offend his partner. Even though he may feel assertive in his demands, he apologizes for the least mistake, and may not show any anger when he is really angry. Timidity can be mistaken for humility or being unintelligent. But it is not true! A timid partner can maintain healthier relationship, but needs to sit up and squarely face the challenges of his daily life. (iii). A *sensitive* personality refers to a serious-minded partner who may have the tendency to take offence for the least provocation. He restrains from cracking jokes to avoid being hurt or upset, and such partners easily get embarrassed when confronted with their ugly behaviors. We must note here, that sensitivity in this sense is just a sign of fear to realistically face oneself and challenges. To get along with them, always read their lips and faces. (iv). An *anxious* personality is apprehensive, feels insecure, tense, always worried over trivial matters and constantly looking for reassurance. This mentality shows a sign of insecurity. The habit to seek reassurance, as noted earlier, creates problems in relationships. This personality seems to correspond to what Agwulonu refers to as a person of choleric temperament such as: "A strong-willed, self-sufficient and very independent. He is quite domineering and self-opinionated, even deciding for others. An old poetical work describes a choleric as a man who fiercely kicks a stone, which lies in his way" (2001:75). Such a partner is always presumptuous and hardly forgives any wrong his partner once did to him; thereby create problems in their marriage. To relate well with such people, avoid any form of argument with them. (V). An *obsession-driven* personality refers to partners or people who are very meticulous and over-conscientious as regards their ways of life and habit, paying attention to minutest details of events and get offended when their plans are interfered with. A partner can be so obsessive over a particular habit, feeding or dressing habit that he hardly keeps to any appointments on time. They have the "it has to be that way all the time" attitude. They are unduly rigid and insatiable. For instance, a husband of an obsessive mentality may not understand why his wife goes to market every day, even though, he loves to enjoy the fresh perishable vegetables she cooks daily. To live and keep up with such people, their partners must have to go extra miles. (vi). A *hysterical* personality is excessively commanding, demanding attention and trying to dominate with some superficial type of emotions. He cannot attend any social function unnoticed. Hysterical partners have sanguine temperaments (from Latin word *"sanguis"* meaning blood) because they are extroverted, buoyant, and lively. According to LaHaye: "A sanguine personality always enters a room with mouth first. His noisy blustering, friendly ways make him appear more confident than he really is but his energy and loveable disposition get him by the rough spot of life. People have a way of excusing his weakness by saying: 'That's just the way he is" (1988:26-27). Though, a hysterical personality is responsive, compassionate, enthusiastic, a talkative, a friend of all, he seems to relate well with everybody. At times, he can be unreliable, forgetful, egocentric and exaggerative. For instance, a hysterical personality may not be as generous to his family as he appears publicly. Such partners tend to hide their true identity, indicating that there is no perfect person in marriage as to claim a capital "P" or Partner in it. (vii). A *Schizothymic* (Introverted) personality loves solitary life, has difficulty to make social contacts, reserved, at times intelligent, and sounds shy, calm and unexcited. This corresponds to "phlegmatic" temperament. In Agwulonu's view: "The phlegmatic is calm, quiet, easygoing, dependable, objective, diplomatic, efficient, organized, practical and humorous. For his weakness, he is unmotivated, procrastinator, very selfish, stingy, self-protected, indecisive and fearful (2001:76). Relationships may experience some Bomb Shells or emotional tensions here when the extroverted live with introverted partners. Introversion can 'exclusively be a sign of deliberate irresponsibility' in relationships. Partners have the tasks to study themselves more. (viii). A *Cyclothymic* (Extroverted) personality, like the hysterical, is an outgoing and outspoken person, warm and friendly. But such people can be so boastful and flamboyant, that often, they may not have enough resources to meet up with their actual needs and pledges. The extroverted must be cautious of what they say and do in their marriage because *"virtus est stat"* - virtue stands in the middle of a vice. (ix). A *Paranoid* personality is always suspicious of others, very careful in the choice of friends. This corresponds to "melancholic" temperament. According to Aqwulonu: "A person with melancholic temperament is: Analytical, self-sacrificing, 'industrious', gifted, 'aesthetic', perfectionist type and are very sensitive to situations…. Given easily to contemplation and introspection, careful in his choice of friends, clothes, and all…neat to a fault and seldom welcome criticisms…for his weakness, he is moody, self-centered, persecution- prone, revengeful, touchy, theoretical, unsocial, critical, negative and scrupulous (2001:75-76). For instance, in marital relationships, a paranoid personality can always provide enough money for the house, but lacks the patience to listen to the feelings of his family. The irony of this situation is that the paranoid is already suspicious of being blamed for lapses when he has not been accused. A paranoid personality needs self-supervision, to trust himself and believe that nothing is permanent under the sun and that no life is perfect or more precious than his and family. Partners of these kinds of relationships must develop more hard skins, positive attitudes; pay less attention to side comments in order to cope with their situations, lots and ride on. Some of these paranoid and anxious personalities really need to be subjected to psychological evaluations before they are assigned public offices! At this most sensitive step in life/ marriage, our MG warms partners of this nature, to avoid allowing their hearts become wastepaper baskets or dustbins for nursing and dumping anger, frustrations and jealousy. Rather, let their hearts become a box of treasure, storing only but love, joy, unity, forgiveness and peace!

14. WISDOM

Wisdom is both a gift and success. Partners are called to apply creative intelligence and caution in their marriage. Wisdom, again, is knowledge of oneself. For instance, when cases of good judgment abound, a partner should posses that quality of discernment, and act creditably. Dalrymple Theodore, reflecting in his work on Shakespeare, noted: "Shakespeare reminds us of the line between good and evil running down the center of all human beings" (IR). Therefore, partners should constantly reason together and monitor this line in order to avoid strife in their marriages and maintain some equilibrium. Each partner is his or her own personality and survival. The "grace and strength" for a woman or man to get married or be married to someone else, with a total different culture, family, state of life, et cetera, entails some radical decisions, courage, determination and humility on that very individual. That is why, to find a life partner is more precious than gold! It does not depend on a person's level of education. Some people may reject it. But, all in all, the ability for you, partners to always reason and "do what you are doing" (*age quod agis* – Latin) with no equivocations, concentrating on doing the right thing at the right time is pricelessly recommended. Thus, couples should be wise enough to read every hand writing on the wall. Always observe your partner's countenance and re-adjust yours, if need be. For, wisdom encourages everybody or spouse to speak the language of humanity – "PLT' (Peace, Love and Tranquility). Never ever allow Satan celebrate your marriage! Be wise enough, because some historical antecedents have shown that your likely, worst or most heartfelt enemy in life might emanate from your own closest group, associate or, even "family".

15. EMOTION

The first thing couples should study about themselves in marriage is the emotional behavior of each other. For instance: "How does my wife feel when I do this or that? Is she the jealous type? Every husband must reason that way to maintain peace in his house. Or, "what does my husband dislike? Does he feel okay when I laugh or play with other men?" A good wife has to reason that way to retain her husband's love. It is normal for partners to be jealous of each other, especially where there is the love that counts no error. Therefore, couples should do the mathematics to avoid offending each other, incorporating their every day way of life, being fully alert to control their feelings towards more joyous fulfillments. An emotionless partner is as good as dead! Naturally, partners can abruptly react to positive or negative stimuli that can encourage or destroy their marriages due primarily to some overwhelming events confronting or facing them in their lives. Yet, the management of one's emotions is success! Take it easy, one step at a time!

16. AGE

Naturally, age is a priceless piece of reality that moves each created being from one life setting to another. For many partners interviewed: "Active prayer life keeps our marriage together". After all, "age is just a number" people say. We can calculate, name, and measure it, yet, it defiles our understanding. For instance, a ten year old child can excellently perform and achieve great heights in academics, arts and other fields which a 30 year old adult cannot. The law of a country can fix and define the age when marriage should occur, but nature, most often, violates it to our surprises! Age in marriage defiles reasonability and common sense! For instance, a young girl of 14 can decide to marry a 65 year old man who is even older than her own ground father and still bears a child for him. However, age affects the mental and physical ability of couples. When that young girl of 14, for instance, marries that 65 year old man, it must take some years, time, patience and endurance to properly balance their differences. It equally happens when an elderly woman marries a young person. Based on these grounds, couples should always be ready to study and pardon themselves when age pushes each other to make certain mistakes.

17. UPBRINGING

A husband may not be justified to scold his wife for not cooking well, for an example, when the parents of his wife had maintained different cooks or maids all her life. Besides, a girl brought up in the city or urban environment should not be expected to behave immediately as the one brought up in the rural community. These traits, idiosyncrasies and cultural milieu affect every marriage. Therefore, couples should take cognizance of these differences to make rooms for mutual tolerance and harmony. The upbringing of children is always meant to be a joint venture, but, more often than not, this expected value or future of children precariously appears to hang on a balance. Yet, the consequences of such half-baked children become the problem of society, because nobody can expect such broken families always to reliably produce children worthy of trust. The Christian Bible put it better: "No good tree bears bad fruit, nor does a bad tree bear good fruit" (Luke 6:43). This is a serious warning to couples who engage in bearing children without any plans to raise or care for them. In support of the above challenging responsibility, two famous psychologists, Hilgard and Atkinson explained it in these words: "As a child comes to seek approval and to avoid disapproval, he begins to see himself as a responsible agent. He develops a conscience whereby he judges his own conduct according to the ideas he has acquired (Op .Cit., p. 645).

These "ideas he has acquired" are contagiously the bone of contentions. Therefore, the environment in which a child grows has much influence in the formation of his or her personality or conscience and the nature of relationships he or she might likely keep. While it is true that a kid may not follow adult conversations, she can easily interpret them! No wonder then, Onwubiko, sounded these serious remarks: "The effects of childhood experience do not end with childhood; it extends to adulthood even to old age" (2007:78) relationships. That old adage equally goes well here: "However a tree stands so does it fall" To make sure the tree falls on the right spot, the warning of an American-based intellectual, once the President of the National Council of Catholic Women Organization of Nigeria, Dr. Nwachukwu Udaku, on social media must be taken so seriously here: "Sometimes, the negative impacts from movies and television can be immediately noticed, for example, when your child sees movies that are heavily laced with violence or pornographic and indecent scenes, expresses or experiments what he had seen during play and association with peers. Other times also the impact may be remote though not so immediate or obvious, it occurs slowly as the child keeps such images over and over again, especially when for example, smoking and hard drugs, sexual irresponsibility are shown and rewarding without showing at the same time the consequences arising from each of these habits (2009:66-67). No child becomes disciplined if left unguarded and aided!

18. ADVICE

There is no advice that is convincing, fruitful and lasting than the ones couples give themselves. Outsiders may use force to restore harmony among couples. But, I believe this may succeed at the theoretical level. Only the couples decide to live as husbands and wives! Therefore, couples need more of our prayers than advice that can be at times, deceitful. It is sensible to note that the advice partners privately give to themselves, we repeat, effectively carries more weight than those that are given by their acquaintances. In the words of Kate Relling Garskot, for instance: "Advice is often a vote of no confidence in the ability of others to solve their own problems" (NYUMC, 2/11/09). Partners solely decide whether to move forward or backward in their marriage! While outsiders are always welcome to advise partners when they feel the need, but they should stop there and never press further to have their advices implemented. Decision ultimately lies on the partners to filter the advices and decide what to do with them.

19. SEX

This is most sacred in marriage. No single partner has any autonomy over it! It is an exclusive right of each of them. The issue should not be raised among couples when any of them has animosity for the other. Settlement is necessary first! That is why rape is completely forbidden in marriage. Couples should always accept whatever reasons their partners may hold as an excuse. Good to note also that the nature of men differs from that of women. Men are easily aroused and satisfied than women. No partner should be anxious or in a hurry over sex, please. Thus, sex should be approached with respect and love. This may eradicate quarrels and infidelity. Summarily, couples should not expect sex from their partners when they are indisposed, weak, sick, tired or undergoing a spiritual exercise, even though, spirituality incorporates the minutest details of all we do as humans. But, do not pretend! After all, certain forms of madness become normal (natural) in the face of sex and money. Again, the term "sex", that spirit-high way, may sound so simple to define than seemingly rushed, approached and understood today. For me, this ageless reality lacks a single definition. In today's world, many tend to run crazy about it, not realizing where it may land or lead them, either to mischievousness, total self-destruction and unfulfilled life dreams or to their untimely deaths. Thus, the mystery of sex lies on the fact that it hears all languages but speaks only one, "let's go!" Sex may oblige all commands, genders, social positions and religions, but it irrevocably remains deaf, unstoppable and unbending on its final judgments.

Ironically, the ever welcoming sex is never a respecter of any human being, be the person a Minister of any religion, President of any country, the most Influential Personality in society, the Richest or Poorest Person on the planet. That is why sex should NEVER EVER be the primary objective for any young man or woman to jump into any unexamined relationship, friendship or marriage. On the same par, while some may freely customize on sex, trade on it, make fortunes with it or risk losing all their savings in life, some divinely use their bodies (sex) to praise and glorify their God! Conjugal relation and family planning, especially in marriages are designed by destiny/God. This is precisely why rape and fighting are completely forbidden in marriage. As the American slogan goes, 'making love in empty stomach' is not acceptable! The "empty stomach" here may not point to physical hunger. The sacredness of sex must be underlined, obeyed and complied with, before it commences. Partners must always try and pay urgent attention to each other, especially when there is need for them to talk first. Yet, rape can be of two distinct types, all pointing majorly to male partners. If a husband or wife gets aroused, it is totally normal. It is not sinful at all! Every healthy, even mental (insane) man or woman feels that way, most often, without any intention for sex as such. A married man should equally and always learn to control himself when such arousals occur. Always take note that the urge or appetite for sex is cravingly, first in you, and may not be otherwise! Thus, a person who can't control his sexual urges is totally not fit for marriage or religious life! Again, sex becomes a rape when the husband forces or bounces on his wife without her consent, often, claiming that, if she refuses to succumb to his demands, whims and caprices, then, she must be after or following other men! Wow! This is not true, man! Sex alone is not what marriage is all about! Also, there can be rape when partners have agreed to have sex. In this sense, the husbands must not be so quick to satisfy themselves first, leaving their wives half-way or unsatisfied as abandoned yesterday's news paper. During those six years of my ministry or advocacy as Judge in the Diocesan Marriage Tribunal, of Ahiara in Nigeria, (without any degree in Canon Law, let alone an experience in marriage) most wives bitterly complained about these aspects of sexual insensitivity on the part of their partners, which, as they singularly remarked: "If not for the sake of having children and my marriage vows, there is no way I would have ever allowed 'that man' to touch me again – imagine, no passion, with tiny, size-less and stingy manhood too. What a torture in my sex life!" Some of these female partners have, even, extended and carried their animosity or anger over to their little babies, abandoning or caring less about them, as serious warnings and retaliation of the foolhardiness, call it, heedless and reckless attitudes of "those men", meaning their partners. At this juncture, I suggest that, husbands should always and thoroughly reason with their wives about how they feel in such sexual relationships, bearing in mind that rape outside wedlock also, which 'was not handled in this Marriage Guide is evil. These days, some husbands have indirectly forced their faithful but aggrieved "wives" into adultery and infidelity due to their nonchalant attitudes and crudeness on the matter. Sex in marriage is not a TV set you can just sit down and watch! Dynamically, it has a divine mandate! Like a valued TV, please, always be genuine and respectfully conscious of when or how you switch it on and turn it off. Always change your sex batteries, and care more! My man! Always be ready and prepared to deliver, when called upon and stop finding baseless faults with your innocent partner.

20. CHILDREN

These are God's gifts and part and parcel of the fruits of marriage, whether born or adopted. For most Igbo people, children constitute the end of marriage! But, this is not necessarily true! In many families today, couples play politics over their children, campaigning to win their love, especially when progress has surfaced in the family. Could economy be responsible for this mess in marriage? Couples should never, for any reason, use their children as escape goats to settle their misunderstanding. Rather, teach them to respect people, society and their God. They should be gladly welcomed into healthy environments and human society. That is why it is so vital to catch them young, assisting them to appreciate themselves, their families and those around them. For instance, a child who has not witnessed bullying or cheating in its family, may not ever engage in such objectionable acts. Give every child the chance to live and never take the divine law into your hands! That abortion is legalized in many parts of the globe today does not make it morally acceptable by everybody. In her own words: "Has anyone reasoned thus: "If our parents had aborted us, I mean, when life was safer, what do you think could have been our fate today?" (Retired Headmistress, Mrs. Rose Nwachukwu). Every child whether born by a teenager, prostitute, lunatic, found in a gutter, abandoned in a dustbin, remains God's handiwork and must be protected. Mothers have greater responsibilities here. As Erikson puts it: "At birth...the child's interaction with the world...is preverbal in nature... and its needs...totally depends on the mother" (1950, in 1967:20). For instance, as observed by Ekeagba: "When you tell your child, 'don't steal', you are helping him to develop superego" (1994:6) or conscience, because superego is the moral arm of the personality. As Dr. Nwachukwu Udaku would have it: "Children and teenagers are very receptive as far as learning is concerned. Little wonder, parents and reasonable adults are very cautious of their actions before them. Their sensitivity is higher than that of our modern day recording devices, and their senses and memories are quick to note, grasp and properly save whatever they observe. These, whether good or bad, later, begin to play out in the course of their growth" (2009:65). Take note!

21. CHARACTER FORMATION

It is always advisable for couples to model their marriage pattern on those marriages (Poor or Rich) that have been proved in their community as successful, exemplary and encouraging. To achieve these, couples must always reason together! Always avoid him or her, no matter how good, close or friendly, whom your partner "hates". Please take note of that! Partners are the organic, motivating force and arms of society. As such, any deflation or erosion on their marriage affects the larger human community in a more drastic manner/way. They need our support and prayers! Thus, character formation does not start one day or at marriage either. It is essentially brewed right from childbirth, nurtured and diligently masterminded to adulthood, incorporating individual states of mind, application of ethical principles, personality types, structures, temperaments, defense mechanisms in relationships, et cetera. That adage which says: "Where a tree bends, is where it likely falls" as already noted in this Life Guide," flawlessly describes 'character formation'. This 21st step is decisively the springboard of the nature of marriage which the partners present to the outside world. It is challenging! Character psychologically refers to the life of a particular person who is now getting into marriage. The questions that spring up here include: "What are those various packages you have acquired or imbibed since birth, how have they patterned your life, feelings, decisions, and reactions to events of life and how are they going to make any difference in the packages your partner may hold for you?" I recommended that we keep praying for these partners. But, another vital question is: "Do these partners really need our prayers as of now, especially as adults?" Yes! Partners need lots of help to thoroughly look into themselves, put on their thinking caps, overhaul every area of past or present unhealthy associations, weaknesses and learn to forgive themselves of silly mistakes they might have made, and begin to learn the language of marriage and redress from their negative life styles, gradually and together, build up an enviable marriage. Some couples tend to blame God when things go wrong, but fail to thank Him when things are progressing. Yet, they fail to note that they are the architects of their woes!

22. PARENTAL CARE

If having children at all is desirably necessary for the couples, to train them should exclusively be their primary assignment. However, the economy of every family determines what may happen here. But, 80% success lies more on the children than on parents, because disciplined children are less expensive to train than decedent ones. However, parents should gratefully shower love and concern on their children. Msgr. Walter Neibrzydowski, my one time Pastor, once said in his 'You Tube Channel @ www. youtube.com/frwalter1& Manhattan Cable Show, Channel 57, Time Warner, Channel 84 RCN, Tuesday @ 10:30 AM' that "We can no longer fold our hands and watch our children perish in social and domestic violence". Partners need to prepare well for parental responsibilities because "it takes more (sacrifices) to be a parent than make a baby" (Oprah Winfrey). Always be careful in relating with kids! In the case of the children of separated parents, for instance, the emotional and heavy weight of their parents' rancor and acrimony lie on them. No wonder Whitehead Barbara once remarked: "In the divorce literature, however, children inhabit a shifting and uncertain social world" (1997:126). In this case, spiritual psychology tries to assist these children of 'uncertain social world' to understand, positively appreciate and identify themselves in the sensible world. Therefore to relate well with kids, give them enough space to get themselves together, always be aware that a lot of things go within them. Involve them in any conversation, event or activity that concerns them, allowing them play some role models and carefully and spontaneously pick, build on their interests, and follow their lead (Cf. pds.kids.org). For instance, kids that have lost a parent, either through untimely death or divorce, normally seek immediate attentions, easily get angry or tend to feel disappointed with the world. They are not to blame because there is no other way to express their feelings. Thus, the best response to this situation by caring partners or parents is not to get angry about the kid's seeming strange behaviors but to invite them to talk about the loss or divorce. Every moment with kids at this tender age has long impacts on their future and character formation as Dr. Oliver Onwubiko noted already. Even in the Catholic Church, the impressions Pastors create to children during their first involvement at the Sacrament of Reconciliation/Confession/Grace, which is never limited to forgiveness alone but to strengthen them up to be better individuals, may encourage or discourage them for life with the Church.

Again, reinforcing children for every little effort they make motivates them to try many other possibilities. Have we all not observed that kids came into this world with great joy? They expectantly show this by looking at the faces of adults to share the same unconditional love with them and begin to learn the principles of earthly and happy life. Unfortunately, most of them quickly fall victim to the sins of parents and society. For the preverbal infants, partners should use eye contact, reading, touching, singing, clapping hands and massaging to communicate with them. In using the eye contact with them, always try to follow their gaze, trying funny, different things and do not keep them on one activity for so long because they easily get bored. Always allow them to have enough rest! It is always phenomenal and monumental to allow kids perceive your positive sides, smell and feel your warmth and love than watch their parents quarrel or bitterly exchange words. Small children within their 'id' personality stage grow with both the positive and negative impressions they made early in their lives and tend to forget most of their childhood memories as they grow older, because they mainly and only care for themselves. Adults, especially parents must generally avoid any scandalous activity before their children. As observed in this Guide, kids may lack the power of words, but they interpret and take note of all facial expressions, moods, movements, tone of words, feelings etc. Unknown to most partners or parents, all these negative acts have great impacts on their character formation and relationships later in life. Babies in their mother's womb equally feel the warmth or hatred of their parents before they are born. Avoid frowning your face when interacting with kids except when they do something wrong. Generally, kids have no malice, prejudice or hatred for any one because they have not yet, imbibed that from the adult world. It is only when society furnishes them with her ills that they begin to express ill feelings. For instance, people have the right to make their decisions, but often, they lack the ability to control the consequences of their decisions. Moreover, on no condition should a parent or partner make jokes or caricature of his or her partner's stature, height, weight or ugly looks, in public. But they can always suggest to each other the best ways to keep fit and healthy.

23. HOUSE HELPERS/MAIDS

Couples should first of all agree to have maids, specify their duties and the condition of their services before they are brought into the house. Most often, especially these days, maids constitute great obstacles to marriage. If possible, let grown up ones be settled for good. On no accounts should maids enjoy the privacy of couples or be employed in the house as spies. But remember, children easily learn more from maids than from their parents.

Thus, couples should treat maids as their own children also. While house helpers must be treated as part of the family, partners must keep very close eye on them because their family training might probably be different. Yet, when maids begin to raise eyebrows, it might mean that "the monkey hands have infiltrated in the partners' relationship. In this instance, nature will not forgive any family, where one partner alone decides what gender of a house help should be employed. The two must express their joint need to have one and what gender to bring in, without raising any voice on each other!

24. FAITHFULNESS

In marriage, love proceeds fidelity, which may include: the hardships, sacrifices, crosses etc., couples are prepared to suffer or carry for the sake of each other. But, it is painful that some couples indulge in unfaithfulness as revenge or corrective measures for the offences their partners have committed. Brothers, be careful here because unfaithfulness is more on your side than on women! Take note, a woman's heart is the deepest ocean of secrets. Be careful! This matter is as sensitive as marriage itself, because no man takes it lightly with an inquisitive wife, who, not only monitors but also exposes his relationships with other women. Behaviors of this sort have shamefully led some husbands take extreme positions that scattered their families. Real love covers unfaithfulness, if any! Marriage is more of, an inevitable link that connects God and man. In this sense, it represents the Domestic Church. Has any partner meditated on why Jesus' First Miracle in human history took place within a marriage feast in which a woman, Mary, ordered or rather launched Him into His 'hour', Who, hearing the voice of His Father re-echoing in His Mother's, commenced His unprepared heavenly task that very moment (**2:**

Jn.4-6)? It is only in marriage that a person can radically and totally change his or her status, life styles and preferences. Let no partner mess it up because fidelity is a universal value that is not only limited to carnal relationships. It is an offence against one's nature, conscience and being to be unfaithful to one's commitment. That was mainly why Burdette noted: "It is not the experience of today that drives men mad. It is the remorse for something that happened yesterday" (1997:147). Oblige me to lend you my motto: "Discipline is doing the right thing when no one is watching you" and this very motto has saved me from numerous and unfounded accusations by individuals who do not know me. Again, hard work and humility are signs of true relationship! Every vocation in life, particularly in marriage, either with a spouse or the Church, demands transparence, constancy and dedication. Therefore, it is deadly wrong for a partner to base his judgments of marriage on rumors and hearsays that have no *locus standi* or verifications. For instance, those wives or women who readily greet people with hugs may be the most faithful ones. That is why fidelity in marriage should not be limited to sex alone. Faithfulness in marriage survives and leads sex and not the other way round. It is only within this understanding that marital relationships can survive affairs. According to Herbert George in Yancey's book: "He who cannot forgive another person breaks the bridge over which he must pass himself" (1997:82). To be faithful is divine and to culture a forgiving spirit is life! Faithfulness is the heavenly ID Card/Visa!

25. GOOD HEALTH

Good health is a gift from God. But, some couples can turn it into a curse. Remember, it can be withdrawn any time, anyhow! Therefore, couples should maximize it to praise God, advance society and enjoy themselves. Do not use it to make cases.

Marriage always comes with many packages that gradually unfold with time. No one ever doubts that good health in marriage or in life is of incomparable importance. Thus, while the 'Dictionary.com' may define 'good health as "the general condition of the body or mind with reference to soundness and vigor...soundness of body or mind; freedom from disease or ailment: to have one's health", this Guide emphasizes more on the soundness of the mind. As the Latin adage has it: *"Mens sana in corpore sano"* that is: "A sound mind in a healthy body". Literally, explicating that a sound mind inhabits and functions in a healthy body. Surprisingly, to the contrary, as witnessed today, a very healthy person or partner may sound sick to his roles in the house. Again, procrastination to urgent needs of the family is a form of in-health. An adulterous or lazy partner, who is not ready to quit or work for their living is deadly sick. In other words, good health is primarily meant to be maximized for the overall joy, peace and progress of the family and never to be compromised for selfish ends! Therefore, partners should work hard with good health, create harmony, cooperate with each other, eat good food within their resources and enjoy good health in their marriage.

26. HARD WORKING

Marriage is joyous and most enviable when couples cultivate the grace of hardworking. A lazy wife or husband makes frequent and unnecessary demands from the other. Some lazy wives resort to having babies yearly. This is no solution! Laziness is a threat to marriage. Therefore, couples must, not only look for a job but, work hard to earn their living. For, idleness is sickness and death. A lazy person may not be good at anything and should not marry. In brief, he is a threat to relationships! He can hardly make any substantial contribution to peace, unity; love and progress that energize conducive relationships. A hardworking partner can always cover up the material lapses that often pledge many families. Being out or loss of job has nothing to do with laziness. Circumstantial situations are normally expected in any marriage and can easily be handled whenever they occur. But, to put up with a lazy partner is dangerously a big risk. Therefore, young men and women are hereby advised to wake up, work hard in their studies, educational fields, and prepare themselves well, if they ever wish to marry or get married, to avoid becoming a nuisance and embarrassment to selves, the Church and society.

27. PRIORITY

This is a matter of common sense. Couples should view their problems from one eye. The need to accomplish common interests is what counts here. Let them have plans. How can a demand of shoe be made when the family has no food to eat? Let no partner test each other's love. Couples should try and solve what cannot be delayed and endure what cannot be solved. Marriage can always survive with little resources, especially where peace and understanding abound! The quest for worldly glories today is not a priority in any marriage. Rather, the weight of one's personality, worth, one's riches and level of one's learning are often evaluated by the nature of relationships one keeps. We cannot solve our problems by running away from them, or talk of doing good when there are evils to be avoided or build healthy relationships in any marriage when old wounds have not been healed. These are the priorities! First things must come first! The care, joy and unity of the partners and family should take the highest priority in marriage. Partners can always learn to start a healthier relationship afresh by first of all acknowledging where each of them has gone wrong. Most often, they create the bad behavior which they tend or seem to encounter and hate in each other. It is better they try to do the good or the right thing and fail than succeed in doing nothing.

28. FASHION

The spirit of fashion or "to match" must be discouraged among couples. They should have tasks to occupy them in the house. Imagine a wife refusing to accept a piece of material her husband bought for her, simply because, it was not current, outdated or gone out of fashion. Of what use is fashion to a struggling family? What couples need is decency and neatness, period! In my own opinion, fashion should go with creativity and innovations. Dancing and singing a particular brand of music, which is popularly and currently out there in society, is not bad at all. This includes the most reigning styles of dress; shoes and ornaments people put on to identify with a particular trend in time. This practice should not be condemned or seen as evil. God, in Genesis, even questioned Eve why she was naked, implying that He had never designed or wished human beings to move around naked! Thus, each partner or person should respect his body and decently clothe it. Regrettably, today, fashion appears to have moved to a brainless dimension or turned into idolatry, where some partners, in trying "to match with the present trend" lavish their hard earned money on expensive clothes, shoes and flashy cars, when, in actual fact, the family is just struggling to put food on their table. Placing greater attention on fashion than facing the family responsibilities is sheer madness. Above all, partners should control their passions, as regards what they wear, put on and eat, period! Sincere Partners enjoy what they have as fashionable!

29. FEEDING

Food is basic to life. The available partner should try and prepare good food for the family and on time too. It is senseless for any partner to start playing jokes with the other when he or she is hungry or in a dirty environment. Unlike in most African countries where only the women own the kitchen, do the shopping, cook the food and serve the entire family. Though, men are expected to provide the resources, but in many cases, it does not follow that way! In this instance, it did not matter if the women had been working all day long, while the men sat idle, doing nothing! The women would be scolded if they delayed serving the food. Even when a man's wife was sick or very tired, finding an alternative was completely off the table. She has to prepare the food! The men would not want their age mates to laugh at or call them names. Thanks to the western world, some senses are gradually being taught into the men worldwide, where everybody has to cook, even a Catholic Bishop! Unlike in Nigeria, where every Rectory or Bishop Court has a paid Cook. To see a priest cooking, let alone a Catholic Bishop, must be the strangest scene ever! Let us take it that Mr. Wow is from Nigeria, besides the fact that his age grade members will laugh at him for cooking on behalf of his sick wife, why cannot he be reasonable enough to realize that the health of his wife is at risk and defile all odds and try the cooking? This is where common sense is paramount in marriage. A husband or wife must face difficult challenges, which he or she could not have ever imagined if still single. Marriage comes with a different package that may not sound pleasant to both partners at times, yet, they must peacefully accept them. A partner loses nothing when he suffers or accepts humiliation to achieve peace in his family. Closely considered, what of when the food items are not available or affordable? Who bears the blame? That kept apart, how can the same husband who dislikes "vegetable" soup in his house, enjoy it elsewhere? Remember, no family has survived without a cross! This is fundamental to life, to start with! In marriage, to feed is not the same thing as to eat food. Eating is a biological and divine requirement which is extended to every living organism. There is no limit to what we can eat and drink! In other hand, to feed includes human participation of the earthly and celestial banquet. We eat to satisfy our appetites and quench hunger to stay alive. Most often, partners, not only fill their bodies with food, but also prayerfully feed their souls with praises, songs, music, friendly and encouraging jokes, go on retreats and fast accordingly. While eating can never satisfy our quest to have more of a particular menu, feeding alone, at times, takes care of our bodies and souls. However, partners must try and set some time when they can come together to eat. Within this context too, partners share love and concerns. In this light too, feeding extends to corporate work of mercy, assisting those who have nothing to wear or eat. Feeding the body with food alone and leaving the soul empty of care, love and God's presence are worse than being actually starved.

30. SHELTER

This is most basic to the life of couples. Bad habitation has psychological effects on marriage. It may lead to loss of self-identity, confidence, personality and even sterility. All the same, it is tempting, funny and always not advisable actually to marry without such a provision. Therefore, couples must secure a place, even on renting before they can put up their own building. A room of one's own is better than residing in another person's mansion or having nothing! Shelter in marriage is not limited to the provision of a place to reside or live. It goes deeper than that! Provision of a peaceful environment is more important than silver and gold in marriage. Shelter lacks comparisons in marriage. After all, before any young man ventures to marry, he must have a descent home, where procreation could be possible. People can hurry over their friendships, put up with other friends, reside with parents, rent a little apartment et cetera! However, in compliance with religious expectations, when a man and woman decide to marry, live together as husband and wife, their shelter must be of uppermost importance. No two words about it, because those who live in 'glass houses should not throw stones' to one another. Shelter helps to safeguard the privacy and sacredness of marriage. There is no rush into any marriage which the parties are not ready to sustain. If you have no shelter, don't marry yet! Renting a place to live goes with so many limitations!

31. CHANGE

Each partner should be conscious of the fact that life is never static. It moves! Change challenges every nook and cranny of life. In marriage, it has got to do with the normal routines and conveniences of a husband and wife. Some married men may have to keep awake throughout the night when they mostly needed sleep because of one unavoidable distraction or the other. Couples starve at times to feed their children. Decorations in the house also go with time. Therefore, couples should welcome change as progress to a better tomorrow. This is inevitable in relationships! To change the bad manners of your partner, you must change your own first; adjust your attentive listening habits and the tone of your unfriendly responses to his or her concerns. Trying to fix your partner's behavior makes no sense when you have not even examined or understood yourself. The marriage of two individuals – a man and woman, does not give immunity or indemnity to one person alone! Individuals poised for marriage must engage themselves in one marriage instruction programs or the other to learn more about what it means to give part of one's self to another person before ever they think of getting married or being married. Adopting the Heraclitian and Tillichian (Internet Resources) ideas of the paradoxical co-existence of the good and bad, opposites also and necessarily exist in a seemingly fulfilled marriage, because, married life is an ongoing process governed by elements of change.

A notorious worst partner today can turn out to become a saint tomorrow. Do kindly read the life of St. Augustine! As you devote some time to study yourselves, pray more often, and, at the same time, work on your personal growing edges! It may sound funny, but it is so vital to note here: "A new Metal has been introduced to Chemistry. The Name is: Woman; The Symbol: WM. The Atomic Mass: Highest when 1st found... tends to get heavier with time; The Physical Properties: Boils at any time, but can freeze at any time, and Melts if treated with love, Very bitter if mishandled. The Occurrence is: Very harmful to you if she sees you with any element similar to itself" (WHATSAPP, 05/26/18). Thus, changes in marriage, if well harnessed, can always oscillate, keep and bring the partners' commitments to the desired fruition. Greedy contenders must be careful! A young person who marries a tycoon because of wealth, without first, finding out the source of such riches, may likely but unknowingly, be waiting for an eminent jail sentence in few years time!

32. TIME

Every minute in marriage, optimally counts! It could be the time to rest, eat, work, play or to pray. There is always time for what we need! Idleness in marriage, again, can always result to gossips, hatred, ill-feelings for the other. No time should be put to negative use! Let every couple try to win that marriage bonanza from his or her partner. "Dear, why not come in now and have some rest please". Times are hard for most families today that partners spend more time struggling to pay their bills and put food on the table, and this creates some misgivings in some families. Relationship counts more on the times partners spend together as a family. Therefore, partners must try to request and accept schedules in their workplaces that might help them to spend some times together as a family. Let them be busy with their time, teaching their kids, if they have, the need to study, read their books and do their home works, and stop wasting them on video games and on the TV. That was why, Dr. Nwachukwu Udaku lamented, citing George Garbner, a renowned TV researcher in these words: "The more time one spends 'Living' in the world of television the more likely one is to report perceptions of social reality (that) can be traced to television's presentations of life and society" (2009:71). Partners should not emulate or put into practice, all the indoor-games they see in the world of TV.

On the same par, partners should never waste their precious time on fruitless activities or in organizing how to win a case in their relationship, or lash the last winning blow to each other. Instead of doing so, they should strategize how to accomplish more vital things in life, within the limited time they have and ask themselves some questions. For instance: "At what point in this marriage will my loving partner become my enemy and why?" Partners must be cautious never to give the evil one any place or chance to interfere in their marriage! Just as the evil one keeps reminding each other of all the atrocious and past nasty behaviors of his or her partner and why they should swiftly do something and quit the marriage, why not, at such devilish thoughts, stagnate and keep him - the devil stranded with memories of those old good days when your partner really sacrificed for you, even if it was only one day, did all within his or her power to show you affections, and then retreat for a possible reconciliation. Procrastination is not always helpful in a relationship that counts on the present and immediate results. While healthy relationships may need some distractions at times, disturbances gradually kill.

More importantly, partners should know that time is free but priceless. They can keep, use, own and spend it, because once it is lost, it is gone forever! Every partner is an airplane of its own family! Though time flies, the partners are the pilots! They can decide to land it safely or crash it. The way partners use their time is decisive in their marriage! Time should be the prime focus in every human endeavor. It is more vital or valuable than money, because you can make more money but not time. Time is eternal, a value, and the golden opportunity that perpetually cooperates with nature. We only live our own lives! But we can assist others to live theirs. Often times, we think it is other people wasting our time. But, it is us who give them the permission to do that. And in reality, these 2 people live inside us. Don't let someone be a priority in your life only when you are to him an option. We lose people most important and precious to us because we don't value their time and that is precisely why some partners do not even know how important their partners are to them, until they are gone. Believe it or not, inside us, there are 2 voices. One voice uplifts up, expands us and wants us to grow, but there is another, the one that holds us back, makes us lazy, complacent or self-regarding and restricts our potentials. Besides, every day, from the moment we wake up till the time we go back to bed, there are 2 battles going on between these 2 voices and at the end only one of them wins - especially, the one we listen to the most, the one we feed, cherish and amplify. It is our choice! How we use our time in marriage crucially matters. Again, Life and time are our two best teachers: Life teaches us to make good use of time, and time teaches us to value life (Cf. a WhatsApp's Video Resources).

33. GRATITUDE

For the least thing a wife or husband does in the family, let the other appreciate it. Even, for instance, when the soup is tasteless, a little encouragement may make it better the next day. Besides, may every wife accept with gratitude as the best, whatever gift the husband offers her and vice versa? It could just be a piece of peanut! For, positive reinforcements may encourage desirable behaviors in the family. Safe journey! Every marriage is a celebration of indebtedness and thanksgiving! Even the phrase: "Thank you honey" may cost nothing. But it can profoundly buy or win everything, peace, unity and progress in any relationship. This MG - Marriage Guide has repeatedly stressed the needs and effects of acknowledgments which partners must show to each other for the little help each ever rendered. Unfortunately, some partners feel so busy to do so, while some fall in line, recognize and appreciate the sacrifices their partners make on daily basis to keep their relationships alive and active. Besides, each moment a partner shows gratitude, whether reciprocated or not, he or she unknowingly adds another feather of God's grace to his span of life. Always appreciate who you are to others!

34. JOB OPPORTUNITIES

These may transiently come and go. But, marriage remains! Thus, couples have the right to know the source of each other's income. This noble idea may prove abortive because of greedy partners. My young people, how can you be partisan or a judge in your own case? How can you steal from your own belongings? Maximize whatever you have to support your family. Let the less materialistic, and greedy partner hide nothing from the other so that you may live longer to reap the fruits of your marriage.

Amen! Amen! Tough moments may eventually come and go with events! But marriage is life, permanently celebrated by two individuals, a man and a woman, come rain, come sun! Most often, partners do not control their jobs! On this note, to be occupied or engaged with any source of income is NEVER the liability of one partner alone, unless the issue was jointly settled among the two. For instance, I know of some families in the USA here, where only the men take jobs outside their homes, whereas their wives take care of domestic assignments in their houses. Moreover, many a time, partners have no idea when job opportunities are being advertised or offered. In this situation, this is where family friends and well wishers can play vital roles by informing such partners of some available job opportunities, depending on their fields of interests. It is always very pitiable for both partners to lose their jobs at the same time. Even if they do, they should calmly hold themselves together, and diligently search for one, without allowing such inevitable occurrences of life to set in and create unnecessary tensions whatsoever in their marriage! That is precisely why unemployment should normally, if not always, be anticipated in every marriage. That is why, good management of the family's resources is extremely crucial. No joke about it!

35. SMILE

Really, to smile does not require any method, training or much effort. Yet, it can be medicinal when properly understood. But, unfortunately some couples smile and laugh only when they see visitors or are away from their homes. This is self-deception! Couples owe it to themselves to put up a little smile, even in the face of enormous needs and difficulties. Every sincere smile always generates peace of mind- This is it –o o! *Nkele wuya -oo!* Metaphorically, a smile can represent what is not physically there. People smile for different reasons. Some partners have murdered their spouses with huge smiles. As the Shakespearean Macbeth would put it: "There are daggers in men's smiles" which alluded to his hidden agenda to conceive blood, plotted, and not only handled bloody taggers but also murdered the fictional King Duncan of England because of his greedy to grab power. Such forms of smiles should downrightly be condemned in any relationship, let alone, in marital one! Rather, smiles are very therapeutic and healing than any modern medication. At times, some of those we regard as rich people live on other peoples' sweat and hard work. Partners should always welcome each other's smiles and jointly try to smile away their differences, problems; gladly and speedily reflect on the best options to tackle their immediate needs. All the same, no partner will be happy to smile to the other, especially when his or her demands had not been properly given some attention. Sincere smiles convey the depth of a partner's soul!

36. POSITION

There is no degree of leadership position a husband or wife may be occupying that should make any of them look down on the other. A peaceful marriage has no need for quality or inequality of power. But, couples can cautiously be proud of their positions and achievements, if any. Thus, whatever contributions couples make for the up keep of their family should be seen within the context of the overall happiness that may lead them to eternity in heaven. Marriage does not count or depend on a partner's position, social, political or religious. Rather, it chiefly depends on an unquestionable tolerance. For instance, a highly dignified, respected and placed partner in the Government has no special position in his home. Those auras and paraphernalia of being influential in society have no place in his marriage except to use them to humbly render key services to his family. The only position each partner must struggle to achieve should center on who might gladly bring peace and outweigh the other in rendering unalloyed service to the family.

37. WEALTH

In some cases today, wealth has reduced marriage to nothingness. Hence, divorce has geometrically continued to be on the increase. Beloved partners, as marriage is of divine origin, it must not be measured in terms of affluence, pomposity and ostentatonism. Wealth is a blessing and indebtedness to God and humanity. Use it to help the poor and the Church. But remember: 'Wealth is relative to time, marriage to life'. It can be a curse to some! Choose one. This is circumstantial! Hard work being rightly channeled, with zeal, can lead to wealth. It is often and divinely given to partners for reasons other than their immediate needs and families alone. In the first place, wealth is a gift, meant to be shared with the less privileged of society. For instance, a wealthy partner today can become a nuisance, a serious burden to the family's peace and stability tomorrow. Therefore, partners must remain appreciative of each other and their creator for guiding and bringing them to their present social status, and be humble enough to respect those who have none. Partners can also be so wealthy in charity, love, caring and accommodating each other's faults!

38. EDUCATION

Marriage is a child of common sense and choice, the end result is happiness. Therefore, education becomes vital in marriage only when it helps partners foster more on the same objective. Ironically, divorce and in discipline; increasingly seems to run higher among educated couples today. Life is beautifully an ongoing program of eventualities that graduates in eternity with heaven or hell. To educate your partner, you must, first of all, create an environment or the atmosphere in which he or she is likely to agree with your views because each individual story differs, and every partner behaves true to type. Partners tactfully need common sense to understand themselves in their marriage and not necessarily academic degrees. Marriage does not require special schooling, except for the parties to emulate the exemplary life patterns of other partners who have remarkably and happily demonstrated confidence and steadfastness in their own marriages. Hence, the choice of Marriage Sponsors must be centered on people of proven character!

39. EXCHANGING OF GIFTS

Couples are called upon to live according to their means. Even though, hardship seems to have forced some into adultery, bribery and corruption today. This is against the legacy of marriage! Expecting too much from the world may lead couples into misunderstanding and disappointments in their lives. Therefore, where a particular philanthropist would not want, either, the husband of Mrs. Wow to be aware of his benevolence, then such gifts must be rejected out rightly. It is satanic promising to assist another man's wife when your own may be on fire. Gifts are signs of shared identity, love and care. The exchanging of gifts is glaringly the sign of deep commitment and love! In this sense, such symbolic gifts of love must not depend on ostentatious values or costly items. Being expressed in the continuous tense denotes an unrelenting condition, where partners adopt a non-verbal language to advance and keep their marriage out of danger. Marriage being a compassionate journey, partners must invariably see each other as one in great need of love and care, and approach themselves accordingly. Exchanging of gifts, besides the prime ones demonstrated on their wedding day, partners can decide to exchange rings on weekly, monthly or yearly basis, as they deem fit! Gifts can be anything for them!

40. CONTENTMENT

Surely, the five fingers are never equal. Couples should try and be satisfied with their lots, no matter how little or poor they are. The spirit of competitions and comparisons must not come into marriage. Couples can always emulate the progress of other God-fearing families for the purpose of progresses too, and not to envy them. Do avoid complaints, please! No one partner can have it all in their marriage! Every person on the planet has some broken suitcases. Each person came into the world naked like any other animal. Our dresses or wears only cover the body and not the heart. Thus, relationship is a precious union of ideas, aspirations, hopes, warmth, feelings, and goals, both on the cognitive, speculative, affective and emotional levels. Marriage constantly calls for self-supervision and evaluation! There might not be trustworthy relationships besides the decisions and efforts individuals possibly make about them. In other words, the life of any relationship depends on the values partners attach to it and these values equally shape the manner they approach each other! No matter what image a partner or friend may reflect in our individual mirrors, "our remembered wellness" (1996:25) or the very unique way we consistently and gladly get about accepting and living our lives depends on us. Hence, it is not proper for other people or families to decide how partners should feel about themselves in their own marriage. At times, joy and sadness reside in a marriage, but partners should create the sense of joy and peace by themselves and not by someone else! Always note that individual experiences differ! It is possible that a partner may view an object differently from his partner. Therefore, to condemn a person or your partner because of a single mistake is totally wrong until you have exactly stepped into his or her own shoes yourself.

41. SECURITY

One of the greatest things a man needs on earth is security. The Greeks call it *"conatus essendi"* while Latin, *"habitatus naturalis."* It is a tendency and natural inclination for one to stick to what belongs to one. Couples need this too! On this ground, a man must not make his wife a slave to his parents or antagonize her before others by shying away from his responsibilities. For every married woman has equal ownership and authority in her marital home. Once a husband respects his wife, he must himself command some respect. But, as for those couples who wisely quarrel and disgrace themselves publicly, they are already in hell fire here on earth, without being policed about by anybody. To maintain peace in the house, loving each other, is security per excellence. By security here, this Marriage Guide does not refer to the one guaranteed by the universal law on human rights or the Government. On the contrary, marriage does not necessarily need any law to guide it. For instance, in marriage, the partners alone are intrinsically the population. Only the two individuals involved, understand the weight of it all, where it pinches or not. The allusion that man is a bundle of possibilities is scientifically proved in marriage because an individual is capable of mystification. Moreover, in marriage, a partner alone can constitute a quorum. That is why this MG insists that partners take little things seriously in their marriage because these little things take care of bigger ones, like: "Are you ok? How was your day? You look tired today, are you hungry?

We must reach there! One day at a time! Hot objects surely cool down! God lives! Let's keep moving and so on!" Thus, as each partner has his own unique filters of perception, the other must try to listen, support, protect those visions by jointly focusing more on doing the basics – how do I help my partner put food on the table, pay our bills, assist the less privileged and assure peace in the house etc? Security in marriage is simply creating a genuine shift within each partner to accept the possible and either to change the impossible or just resign to it. There is security when partners view things from one lens, securing themselves in one purpose. That is to say, when partners ultimately insure themselves in their Creator, in their preparedness to accept each other, they eventually bring real value to themselves and to those around them. An unbiased trust to each other is security.

42. CLEANNESS

The ancient proverb holds that cleanness is next to Godliness! Naturally, resourceful women enjoy cleaning this or washing that, while men are generally in a hurry for one appointment or another. All the same, men have their own role to play here. When a man or woman discovers that the partner is dirty and does not care, they must patiently have to endure, tolerate or politely invite each other for joint bathing! Of course, to complain could cause bad feelings. But, unknown to most partners, uncleanness obviously dwindles and diminishes marital love and institutes misunderstanding in the house. On a more serious note, let no partner approach each other dirty. Remember, cleanness is beauty! "Being clean is a sign of spiritual purity or goodness" (IR – Internet Resource). The saying is most relevant in every human relationship, specifically in marriage. No partner should underestimate the need for cleanness, because the growth and decay of marriage primarily depend on it. I have heard it all, as a Judge in marriage cases! Cleanness in marriage is also rewarded! Uncleanness, both on the part of men and women has geometrically led to half of the divorces recorded in the modern marriage. The irony of this vital ingredient of marriage seems to remain a mystery because hardly do partners risk their marriage to inform the other how he or she feels! For instance: "Honey, you need to bathe and clean yourself properly please!" However, this Marriage Guide warns each partner, man or woman: 'NEVER approach your partner, for any sexual relations, without making sure that you have thoroughly washed up!" Women generally hate any smelly partner and vice versa! Besides, tidiness is sacrosanct in marriage! The last partner to get out of bed, (especially where they share a family type), must always try and tidy it up and keep the room in a good going over. Unless a partner is sick, weak or returned very late from work, there are no other reasons for him or her to remain in bed in the morning. Please, get up! Tidy up the room and get ready for the day's business! Such little careless attitudes cause heavy turbulence in marriage! Cleanness here extends to being honest and truthful to each other!

43. POVERTY

Man, by nature, is resistant to poverty. To be in need is not poverty. To be poor in spirit is grace. But, globally speaking, poverty is anti- natural and a form of curse. Some women may prefer to live better with little cash at hand than to talk of love in marriage when the physiological needs are not there. At this juncture, marriage may seem to have been punctured. Yes, it looks some-what true! Put up a little effort still! Be strong! Absolute trust in God, the Miracle worker, works when we cooperate! An antidote within your purse! Surprises in any given marriage are unavoidably important values of life. Partners should always watch out for them and be prepared to contend with them when they spring up. It is not true that poverty ruins every marriage, especially where there is agape kind of love. All the same, to be poor is not the same as being in need. Poverty in marriage can take many forms, namely: 'Laziness to seek any job at all, non appreciation of the contributions of a hardworking partner, being insensitive to the need of the family, giving glimpse excuses to dodge one's responsibility and demonstration of total poor attention to one's partner'. In abject poverty, which could unmanageably occur as a result of natural disasters, partners should hold themselves together first, seek assistance from family members, friends, charitable organizations and international relief bodies etc. But on no condition, should partners ever waste their time in name-calling, blames and agitations. Instead, let them note that 'no condition on the planet is permanent'. Even when all avenues seem to have closed, one's faith and hard work can lead one to many seasons of abundance and plenty.

44. SICKNESS

Nobody prays to be sick! Yet, it must come all the same! Thus, when it happens, couples should not run helter skelter, consulting this Prayer house or that "*dibia*" for solutions. God is the greatest Healer. Seek him at the hospitals and in prayers for assistance. Remember, sickness can equally reshape beauty. Now, when this happens, who recovers or dies; your partner's beauty or the love you hold for each other? Be firm! Humans are imperfect beings! A partner may suddenly fall sick when his or her attention is urgently needed in the family. No doubt, sickness is a serious threat to the partner's peace and a test for real commitment in marital bonds. A caring partner will always and saliently remain supportive and available. In this perspective, to care is to listen empathetically, step up and set out from ones comfort zone and be with the other. Sickness is not the time for name-calling, recounting a partner's failures and weaknesses in the marriage or for the other partner to be rejoicing, singing and dancing! However, prevention is always better than cure! If partners can lessen their demands on each other, for trivial matters the better. Thus, stress being our bodies' response to any form of demands others make on us, the ways we handle them are definitive! We refer to this state of mind as 'psychosomatic' – in which the unpreparedness or unwillingness of the mind to entertain, welcome, even jokes, let alone sex at that moment, makes the body itself so sick. Partners need to recognize the signs of these indispositions and remain sensitive to the feelings of each other! That is to say, whether the partners become sick or enjoy their good health, depends on them! For instance, inasmuch as there is good and bad stress, any partner who jokingly and joyously approaches a hungry or indisposed partner is ultimately creating more stress for him or her and the net result must be ugly felt and regretted. Again, nothing can be more stressful, sickly than a partner ignoring the views of the other and on top of it, tries to create noisy atmosphere, switch on the TV, play music, even to laugh at that moment. Such scenarios lead to frustration and break-ups in many relationships. It does not matter what good, a partner wishes to do for the other at that moment, once she sounds weak or tired, all other actions and kind gestures MUST instantly be suspended. Do also note that laziness and bad life-styles are equally serious forms of sickness. Be mindful that most true lessons of life are not always planned.

C. THE POST LIMINAL STAGE OF THE JOURNEY

45. THE SOCIETY

Nobody is an island! We need others to exist! Though, marriage is one and subjective, it is lived among other people. New married couples can win the admiration of the public only when they are other-regarding and open-minded. The readiness to cheerfully greet and respect others endears many couples to society. As such, when 'the' society welcomes any marriage, the net result will be huge success. The definite article "the" says it all! When we discuss of society in religion, politics or history, we may not specifically be referring to marital relationships, because in marriage, the two parties involved constitute 'society'. That is why family morals are foundational constituents in shaping the nature of any given society and within a particular milieu. For instance, an internet resource may define society as "the *aggregate* of people living together in a more or less ordered community… the *community of people* living in a particular country or region and having shared customs, laws, and organizations…<u>company companionship, fellowship, friendship</u>… a *specified section of a community*…an *organization or club* formed for a particular purpose or activity… the *situation of being in the company* of other people", etc., marital relationships share a unique status. For instance, from the above denotations, marriage, though, being part and parcel of society in general, is solely and decisively an agreement between two separate individuals. Thus, the decisions, choices and behaviors of a single family of husband and wife may affect and influence the large community of people. On the same par, the actions of the members of secret societies, gang groups, terrorists and occultists equally affect society in the most destructive and repulsive manner.

46. PARENTS-IN-LAW

Couples owe it as obligation to assist their parents. However, in most cases, this does not work because of the added -responsibility that has sprung up. Surely, some parents-in-law, even sisters-in-law are impossible to manage. Who can take the risk to educate such parents-in-law, to understand that the innocent young couples are now battling to make ends meet? The issue of charms is always drummed here. My young couple, this is an ugly experience in the married state. Simply encourage each other to be generous and leave the rest to God. For, generosity has a long term benefit. This MG purposefully singled out the conflicting roles these valuable individuals play in marriages today. A parent-in-law who enjoyed their marriage must assist their sons and daughters to enjoy theirs also! While the couples must do everything, humanly possible, within their resources and power to assist their parents, the parents themselves should patiently study and understand the economic condition and stability of their children before mounting unbearable demands and pressures on them. The position of parents-in-laws have precariously become so urgent today, especially in the western world, where they have ruthlessly and ungodly created deep wounds in their children's marriages because of their insatiable cravings. They must reasonably stop such paths to eternal destruction! The partners involved must come together, workout from their incomes and decide the best ways they can assist their parents, save themselves and their parents from everlasting condemnation because of perishable gold and silver! For instance, it is practically hard, if not totally impossible to satisfy a dependent family member, friend, neighbor, partner whose inordinate desires, material expectations and appetites are higher than the source. Thus, getting worried over the attitudes and selfish habits of an unsatisfying or ungrateful partner or person is of no use. Partners must simply try and create some peace and joy for themselves, because they are the only partners who are themselves on the planet. Afterwards, the world is never going to be limited by incessant demands of parents-in-law. Nature remains on its own track and course irrespective of whether we please any one or not. First and foremost, try and safeguard your marriage!

47. RELATIONS

With extended family systems, especially in Africa, some couples find life extremely difficult to cope with. Certainly, couples are bound to receive their relations with open arms. But, some relations, like some parents in-law, abuse these privileges. This is not fair to marriage. Therefore, couples must have to advise themselves first without letting any of the relations either of the husband or the wife, to know of their decision. It has become necessary that relations assist couples and understand that every marriage needs some prayerful atmosphere and quietude. The word 'relation' has many interpretations. A relation could refer to a person's kinsman or woman, a distant cousin, ones sibling, aunt, uncle, niece, or nephew etc. It could also point to a relative, an individual in sexual relationship, correlative, connected and interconnected by blood. In this sense, two people can be connected to each other by marriage. All the same, in this Guide, that the two individuals have agreed to marry; understandably does not raise any problems at all. The troubling cankerworms that deeply seem to corrode marriage are their numerous acquaintances and relatives who perch on them with unmerciful and vested interests. In other words, partners must never prioritize their relatives or extended family members when they have not gathered themselves together from their most pressing challenges or figured out the best ways to tackle them.

48. FRIENDS

Marriage does not require special friends because a friend before marriage may turn out to become the worst enemy after marriage. All the same, we are all bound to pray for the success of every marriage. In this light, couples should not allow friends, no matter how helpful or interested they are in the family, to come very close to their private lives. I repeat, couples should not, under any pretence, reveal to ANYBODY any discussion they hold to be secret. If not, displacement of any member, disregarding of the family in question, is eminently possible, thereby setting the marriage ablaze. Stop coining excuses here! You may have so many friends and associates to back you up to divorce your partner, but, in many instances, when the moment of truth surfaces, none of them may be there, as Fr. Pellegrino J. once observed: "Truth has nothing to do with numbers" (IR, 8/23/09). Even the accepted sacrifices of a single prophet, Elijah and the rejected ones by the 450 prophets of Baal are practical points of reference here (1Kings 18: 20-27). Wishing and praying for a better tomorrow when the advantage of today has not been utilized is ignorantly a waste of time and energy.

49. RELIGIOUS AFFILIATION

The devil appears in diverse colors! Kindly read: "The Divine Deceit: Business in Religion" by Fidelis K. Obiora to discover why marriage needs oneness of mind and purpose. Thus when marriage is not of the same faith, color, culture, and what have you, problems may erupt in the family. But, where mixed marriage is unavoidable, a divine intervention must be sought to bring peace in such a family. Let the couples agree, at least to bring up their children in one faith, if possible. Personally, a person's religious affiliation should not create conflicts in marriage. Even if conflicts and disagreements spring up, they are normal! But, they must be respectfully managed! In the Catholic Church, mixed marriages are allowed and celebrated, mainly between two baptized parties, a Catholic and non-Catholic. Non-religious individuals can still and freely agree to marry in the Catholic Church, through certain laid-down norms and protocols like the RCIA – Rite of Christian Initiation of Adults. Marriage is a sine qua non, so essential before two individuals, a man and woman live together. In my limited understanding and perception of a Merciful God, I don't think God cares so much on one's religion as how the various adherents worship Him in their every day interactions with others, especially today that many Evangelists, heaven-on-earth preachers have tagged God for sale or as a commercial commodity left for the highest bidder, all for monetary profits. Wow! And all in the name of religious affiliations! Shame!

Really, it is heart-breaking to watch the very unique role the Mother Church, Catholic by nature (from the Greek word, '*Katholikos,*' meaning "Universal, all over the world") played through history, particularly by Her Monks, the order of the Cenobites, to preserve the Manuscripts of the Sacred Text/ Scriptures. These included both the OT and the NT, especially from the Very Words of Christ Himself, down to the years between AD 400 and 1450 when Printing Machine was invented by John Gutenberg, which intensified the multiplication and availability of the Bible – the OT & NT, the issue of Canonicity, Division and Inspiration of the Bible notwithstanding! While I do not encourage religious bigotry, to acknowledge the goodness in the other is divine! The open, an unanswered question still remains: "Had the Church, through Her Sacred Tradition (the passing on of the Word from one generation to the next), not preserved and brought most of the Words and Acts, Christ spoke and did to the green light, the OT inclusive, amidst so many persecutions, who could have stood, let alone, risked his conveniences to avail us with the Bible today?" The Gospel of John, Chapter 21, verse 25 specifically underlined it "Had all Jesus did were to be written down, no book on the whole world could have contained them". Thanks to the same Sacred Tradition, we still have some of those words today! Now, how can any modern Bible Scholar justify any position that relegates the same Catholic Church to the background and still claim to have anything to do with the Bible? Well, many do, with heated arguments, claiming the authority and ownership of the Bible, mainly because of our present materialistic culture. My earlier work, published October, 1992, entitled "*Cabia*: The Church and the Bible: Which First?" solely sold in Nigeria, has taken care of these likely informative arguments. The word "*Cabia*" simply means "Please, come". Our point remains: "Instead of religion to divide the family, let each partner stick to his or her own religion and never to allow same to dictate how they relate in their home". Again, let my fellow believers in God, not be surprised that a devoted Atheist, who loves, respects and assists others for who they are may enter God's kingdom before us! James did say it: "Pure and un-spoilt religion in the eyes of God is, coming to the help of orphans and widows when they need it..." (James 1:27) and not the "church" as religion is not always an option for heavenly rewards.

50. GOOD MANNERS

A man, who finds a good wife in marriage, has found himself a treasure. For, goodness begets goodness! Besides, goodness has no measures except those qualities that are generally accepted in society as such. Couples are hereupon called to practise those virtues, which make them acceptable before God and man. Remember, God did not create us, just for marriage. And since the Christian marriage is a Sacrament, we must try and live above the mere coming together or joining up of hands at the altar to radiate the selfless love and sacrifices it holds for society. The toughest steps in every marriage could be the simplest, most blessed and achievable. Society will never be in want of men and women, boys and girls. Yet, every husband is a man but not every man is a husband, just as every wife is a woman, but not every woman is a wife. Thus, do pray for this rare gift of a life partner. Be slow to befriend divorcees or those couples who would prefer their partners dead than alive! In all, good manners only speak in actions. Play your part well, period! Marriage is patch-patch at times! Only God, Who is Completeness, Goodness, Happiness, Success, etc, holds the umbilical cord of every marriage. As repeated in this MG, it is possible that something is eating you up, destroying, and keeping you sad, uncomfortable in your marriage or seems to be diminishing your love for your partner, but, have you ever imagined that, at times, that very thing is you, your unhealthy life styles? Then, for you to break such ugly habits, first of all, acknowledge that there is a problem, which you have unintentionally caused. Why not begin to create the will to act differently? Again, Knaus, citing from the Editors of Bottom Line Publishers, observed: "To break a problem habit, you need to create a 'will to change'…a command effort that allows experimenting with change, accepting its difficulty and moving ahead again even after inevitable backsliding… Deflect your attention from the habit to something else (1998:51). In other words, that 'something else' which seemed to have created problem in your marriage in the past, should never be allowed to play another role in the future. Do remember that the evil ones and our enemies who normally do not rest, or go on vacation, may not know what we have in our minds till we invite them in what we say and do. Discretion is totally needed here, because there may not be a perfect marriage or relationship anywhere. All the same, good manners constitute the kernel and focal line of marriage, and not necessarily outward looks that can be deceitful. As each partner is unique and behaves differently, never give up, constructively building your future, choosing the best path of life that does not, in any form, constitute an obstacle to your marriage or to others and prayerfully follow your heart, always doing the right thing by God's grace.

CONCLUSION

At this juncture, Ladies and Gentlemen, I must confess that I have never been an expert in the area of marriage, with no experience as a Catholic priest, a celibate too. But, my position as Judge in the Marriage Tribunal of my Diocese as noted above, furnished me with enough knowledge to assist individuals in various relationships, especially in married state. Besides these 50 steps offered here, there might have been other important ones I omitted. I call on everybody, especially the married and the young ones, yet unmarried, to try and put these steps into action.

What I told the Senior Seminarians of Bigard Memorial Seminary, Enugu in 1996 when I moderated their annual retreat could apply to married people too. Thus: "Every word, step, action of a rational being acquires its own merits and demerits and is eternally and accordingly weighed". Therefore, let every partner in marriage or any state of life put up his or her best, realizing that a greater reward or punishment awaits all of us hereafter. Be firm, doing what is the best and right!

SOME RELATED-READING REFERENCES

Agwulonu, Fidelis I. 2001. *The Creative Intelligence.* Onitsha: Mid-Field Publishers.

Benson, H. 1997. Timeless Healing: The Power and Biology of Belief. New York, NY: A Fireside Book Publishers-Simon & Schuster.

Carl, Anderson. 2008. *A Civilization of Love: What Every Catholic Can Do to Transform the World.* New York: HarperCollins Publishers.

Chilagorom, Desmond. N. 2006: *Family Life in the Light of the Gospel.*

Erik, H. Erikson. 1980. *Identity and the Life Cycle.* New York: W.W. Norton & Company.

Goldberg, M. & Jay, P. 1983. The Story of Our Values and the Value of Our Stories. MN: Collegeville.

Haughey, C. John. Ed. 1977. *The Faith That Does Justice: Examining the Christian Sources for Social Change.* New York: Paulist Press. *Keeping Human Relationships Together:*

Hawkins, R. David. 2006. *Transcending The Levels of Consciousness: The Stairway to Enlightenment.* AZ: Veritas Publishers

Hayes, M. John. 1994. *Th e Fundamentals of Family Mediation*. New York: State University of New York Press.

Hellwig, K. Monika. 1981. *Understanding Catholicism*. New York: Paulist Press.

Henry, Veatch B. 1974. *Aristotle: A Contemporary Appreciation*. Bloomington: Indiana University Press.

Heraclitus, (Stanford Encyclopedia of Philosophy). *2007. Studies in Heraclitus* by Graham Daniel W.

Heraclitus, (C 536 BC - 475 BC), Talk: *Heraclitus – Wiki quote,* July 2, 2009.

Heraclitus, *Internet Encyclopedia of Philosophy &* in Stumpt, S. E. (1977).

Jamison, Kaleel. 1989. *The Nibble Theory and the Kernel Power: A Book about Leadership, Self-Empowerment, and Personal Growth*. New York: Paulist Publishers.

Johann, O. Robert. 1966. *The meaning of Love*. New Jersey: Deus Books Paulist Press.

John Paul 11. 1995. *Evangelium Vitae*. Vatican: Vatican Press.

Josef, Pieper. 1965. *The Four Cardinal Virtues; Prudence, Justice, Fortitude, Temperance,* (tr. Richard & Clara Winston), NY: Harcourt, Brace, and World.

Karol, Wojtyla, Pope John Paul 11. 1981. *Love and Responsibility.* Willetts H. T. (Tr). NY: Farrar, Straus, Giroux.

Kennedy, E. C. 1974. *The Pain of being Human*. New York, a Division of Doubleday & Company, Inc.

Kilgard, E. R. & Atkinson, R.C. 1967. *Introduction to Psychology 4*th *Edition.* New York:: Harcourt, Brace & Word, Inc.

Kuhse, H. 1997. *Caring: Nurses, Women and Ethics.* Great Britain: Blackwell.

LaHaye, Tim F. 1988. *Why You Act the Way You Do.* Tyndale House Publishers.

Lauder, E. Robert. 1978. *Loneliness is for loving.* Indiana: Ave Maria Press.

Lawrence, J.P. 1972. *Individual Instruction.* London: Mcgraw Hill Book Company.

Mead, S. Frank. 1965. (ed). *The Encyclopedia of Religious Quotations.* New York: Books, Incorporated Publishers.

Morgan, John H. 2006. "Being Human and Being Good: The Psychodynamics of Personhood" (Co-ed). *Religion and Society. Summer Programme in Th eology 2006.* Indiana: Cloverdale Corporation.

Norman, Doidge. 2007. *The Brain That Changes Itself: Stories of Personal Triumphs from the Frontiers of Brain Science.* New York, New York: Penguin Books.

Nwachukwu, Anthony O. 2002. *Salvation in African Context.* Owerri, Nigeria: Barloz Publishers.

_______ 2001. The 50 Steps to Happy Marriage (2nd Edition). Owerri: Assumpta Press.

_______ 1994. *FIRE! The Active Life Of the Spirit.* Owerri: Assumpta Press.

_______ 1999. *The Devil Has Come To Church Part* Owerri: Good Samaritan Press

_______ 1995. What a Model is MARY: The Mother of Jesus. Owerri: Assumpta Press.

Nwachukwu Udaku, Ugoeze, Josephine (edited by Victoria U. Nwigwe). 2009. *The Presidency of Mama JO, Reflections and Adminotions.* Nigeria: NCCWO Publishers.

Obiora, Fidelis K. 1998. *The Devine Deceit Business in Religion.* Enugu: Rex Charles & Patrick.

Onwubiko, Oliver A. 1999. *African Th ought, Religion and Culture. Vol.1.* Enugu: Snaap Press.

Restak, Richard. 1991. *The Brain Has a Mind of Its Own. Insights from a Practicing Neurologist.* New York: Harmony Books.

Romero, Anna A. & Kemp, Steven M. 2007. *Psychology Demystified, A Self-Teaching Guide.* New York, NY: McGraw-Hill.

Shlemon, Leahy Barbara. 1982. *Healing The Hidden Self.* Notre Dame, IN: Ave Maria Press.

Sonderegger, Th eo. 1998. *Cliff s Quick Review PSYCHOLOGY.* NY, NY: Wiley Publishing Inc.

Sue, W. Derald & Sue David. 1990. *Counseling the Culturally Different: Th eory & Practice (Second Edition).* New York: A Wiley-Interscience Publication.

Tillich, Paul J. 1955. *The New Being.* New York: Charles Scribner's sons.

________ 1952. *"The Courage To Be"* An outline edited, Abridged & Expanded by Richard Schwartz.

________ (1886 – 1965). From Contributed Quotations and Lecture by Author.

Ware, Corinne. 1995. *Discover your Spiritual Type.* NY: An Alban Institute Publication.

Whitehead, D. Barbara. 1997: *The Divorce Culture; Rethinking our commitments to Marriage and Family.* New York: Alfred A. Knopf, Inc.

The Catechism of the Catholic Church. 1994. Vatican: Paulist Press Yancey, Philip. 1997. *What's Amazing about Grace?* Michigan: Zondervan Publishing House.

Few biblical references from THE JERUSALEM BIBLE – Popular Edition: London, (ed.) Darton, Longman & Todd, to assist married couples. Please make time to read them, being mindful that marriage journey, once begun cannot easily be dissolved: Gen. 1: 26-28, 2 18-24; Tobit. 8: 4-8; Eccl 26:1-4, 13-16; 1 Cor. 7: 1-40; Eph 5: 2,21-33; 1 Peter 3 1-9: Matt 19: 3-6; Jn. 2: 1-11; Mark10:6-10. Good luck!

APPENDIX A

About The Author

Anthony O. Nwachukwu is Professor of Counseling Psychology and West African Studies and Chair of the New York City Ph.D. Thesis Defense Panel. Father Anthony has also been appointed Consulting Faculty to the Bureau of West African Scholars. His areas of research, writing and teaching include ethics, religion, spirituality and psychology.

Anthony O. Nwachukwu, Ph.D., Psy.D.

Dr. Nwachukwu has taught at Ibiam Girl's High School, Afikpo, Abia State, Nigeria. He has taught Latin in Bigard Memorial Major Seminary (Nigeria) as well as a wide range of courses in religion at St. Peter Claver and Mater Ecclesia Seminaries, both in Nigeria. Ordained a priest in 1987, Dr. Nwachukwu is Nigerian and has served as pastor for thirteen years in Nigeria, during which time he published several works of scholarship. In 2008, he was awarded the Dorothy Day Prize in Pastoral Care and Counseling from the GTF. He holds the B.A. Honors in

Divinity and Philosophy from the Bigard Memorial Seminary (an affiliated institution of the Urbanian University, Rome), the Post Graduate Diploma in Educational Technology and the Master of Education in Educational Philosophy from Imo State University, the Master of Divinity from the Catholic Institute of West Africa, the Ph.D. in Religious Studies from the Federal University of Port Harcourt, Nigeria, and the Doctor of Psychology from the Graduate Theological Foundation (www. gtfeducation.org).

In 2016, Dr. Nwachukwu was inducted as a Fellow of the Graduate Theological Foundation in recognition of his many years of service to the GTF as Professor of Counseling Psychology and West African Studies and in appreciation of his outstanding service as Chair of the New York City Doctoral Defense Panel. Dr. Nwachukwu is a certified Chaplain member of the National Association of Catholic Chaplains and has served for over seven years in the New York University Medical Center, and was the first chaplain to be the recipient of the Safety Team Award by the Nursing Department of the Medical Center. Dr Nwachukwu has recently been certified in New York as a Mediator in Conflict and Resolution, in addition to being a Retreat Moderator, First Assistant Administrator of Mater Ecclesia Diocese, a Theological Vicariate Examiner, and former, Judge in the Diocesan Marriage Tribunal (Ahiara, Nigeria).

Currently, Fr. Anthony is ministering in the Catholic Diocese of Brooklyn, NY, with a welcoming Bishop. Besides his being assigned to extend his pastoral services on part-time bases to few other areas, he is a full time Chaplain of St. Ann's Novitiate – The Little Sisters of the Poor - LSP, Queens Village, NY, where he resides and also enjoys his harmonica. Fr. Anthony embraces this appointment as divinely-directed and his mission in the USA fulfilled and completed. Let us keep glorifying the Lord in the little things we do for ourselves, our spouses and each other! Amen!

APPENDIX B

Books

- Questions and Answers in Philosophy (1982)
- *CABIA:* The Church and the Bible which First? (1992)
- LOVE Biko Bia: Is Love a Risk? (1993)
- Call no one on Earth your Father' Matt. 23:9. Why Rev. Fathers? [1993
- Igba Nkwu Nwanyi (Traditional Marriage) And the Church: Where Stand. A talk first delivered to KSM, Aba Diocese, Nigeria (1994)
- FIRE: The Active Life of the Spirit (1994)
- ENVY: A Deadly Sickness, has only one Medicine (Part 1) - 1994
- What a Model is Mary, the Mother of Jesus (1995). A talk first delive the COMITIUM. The Legion of Mary, Kano State, Nigeria
- Whose Cross and whose Glory? (1996)
- Christ at 2000 Years in Nigeria, Has His Coming Become a Failure: Mary's Apparitions Now?? (1997)
- The Devil Has Come To Church (Part 1)-1998
- The 50 Steps To Happy Marriage (1999) & Reprinted 2001. A talk first to The National Council of Catholic Women Organization of Nigeria
- Salvation in African Context (2002)

- Keeping Human Relationships Together: Self Guide to Healthy Living iUniverse Publishers, 2010 and Reprinted 2011
- GOD CAN BE SO FUNNY: PRIESTLY SILVER JUBILEE PHYSICAL ENCOUNTERS WITH SPIRITUAL FORCES – Bloomi IN: iUniverse Publishers, 2013
- Besides, Fr. Anthony is the Artist of:
- *"Anyi bu ndi otu Christi n'ezie"* And 'Ato *n'ime otu Chineke di Ngozi* the Catholic Teaching on the Most Holy Eucharist and Trinity; An albu tracks).
- "Ewoo, Nne m Maria a muola Onye Nzoputa" (On the Virgin Mary's of Jesus; An album in 6 tracks).
- "Mere m Ebere O Nna" (On the Intercessory Role of Mother Mar album in 10 tracks)

He is also a Mariologist and a Prayerful Advocate of Marian Course, has written a lot of articles, given a number of lecturers to different Christian communities and has, as his motto: "Humility is the sign of Christ's presence, Love of Neighbor - the only sign of a true religion, irrespective of who is involved because Discipline (which is key) is doing the right thing when no one is watching! Sincerely make others happy to be happy yourself". Kindly goggle and read my spiritual testimonies and physical encounters with forces beyond human explanations, published here in the USA by iUniverse, entitled "God Can Be So Funny" and begin to realize why God and His Church must never ever be taken for granted! Church Officials can make mistakes, err, go wrong or sin, but Jesus Christ's Church Herself is infallible! Only God judges unmistakably!